What Jazz Is

What

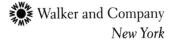
Walker and Company
New York

Jazz Is

An Insider's Guide to Understanding

and Listening to Jazz

JONNY KING

FOREWORD BY CHRISTIAN MCBRIDE

Acknowledgments

Love and thanks to Jacqueline, Sophie, Ed, Ruth, Deb, Jon, Jude, Gid, Zachary, Aliza, Emma, and all the musicians I have played with and been inspired by for the past two decades.

Photographs on pages 2, 50, 90, 106, 118, 130, and 148 copyright © 1995 Mosaic Images. All rights reserved.

Photographs on pages 8, 20, 28, and 76 copyright © 1996, 1997 Jimmy Katz/Giant Steps. All rights reserved.

Photographer Jimmy Katz wishes to thank his assistant, Laura Coyle.

First published in the United States of America in 1997 by Walker Publishing Company, Inc.

Published simultaneously in Canada by Thomas Allen & Son Canada, Limited, Markham, Ontario

Library of Congress Cataloging-in-Publication Data
King, Jonny.
    What jazz is: an insider's guide to understanding and listening to jazz/Jonny King; foreword by Christian McBride.
        p.   cm.
    Includes index.
    ISBN 0-8027-1328-9 (hc)   —ISBN 0-8027-7519-5 (pbk)
    1. Jazz—Analysis, appreciation.   I. Title.
ML3506.K56   1997
781.65—dc21   97-8139
                                                        CIP
                                                        MN

Book design by Lee Fukui

Printed in the United States of America

10   9   8   7   6   5   4   3   2

Make no mistake, this music is for *everyone*! Black, white, young, and old. Jazz is not an exclusive, elite club.

—CHRISTIAN MCBRIDE

CONTENTS

FOREWORD

JAZZ. What an art form. Musicians all over the world are contributing to it every day. Nonmusicians all over the world enjoy it. It's also an art form that some people don't know much about and, unfortunately, don't care to know about! Nevertheless, this art form is a national treasure.

This book will enlighten not only jazz musicians but jazz fans on every level: the Connoisseur, the Fair-Weather Fan, and the MTV Fan who is just starting to listen to jazz. I guarantee that after you read this book, you'll get the urge to run to your nearest CD/record store and buy a few recordings by that "Monk" guy or that "Blakey" guy, or by any of the artists whose names you'll come across here. How do I know?

As a young boy, I vividly remember watching my great uncle listen to his jazz records. This seemingly weird and strange-sounding music would move him to unexpected, abrupt jolts of excitement. He would laugh, swoon, and sometimes dance to it. His passion for jazz made me wonder, What's in this music that's making him go through all these antics?

Though I became curious about his passion, I played it safe for the next few years, listening to Michael Jackson, Prince, DeBarge, and of course the "Godfather of Soul," James Brown. Occasionally, I would still hear jazz music during a visit to my great uncle's or my grandfather's house, on the radio, or on television. I didn't dislike it completely, but I couldn't quite grasp what I was listening to either.

Then when I was eleven years old, my great uncle gave me a record called *Jazz at Massey Hall*. I was told the band on this recording was "legendary" but I recognized only two of the five names: Dizzy Gillespie ("Oh yeah, I saw him on 'Sesame Street' demonstrating how he can puff his cheeks way, way out!) and Max Roach ("I heard Uncle Howard mention him as one of the greatest drummers who ever lived. . . . Is 'Roach' his *real* name?") The others I hadn't heard of were Bud Powell, Charles Mingus, and Charlie Parker. I quickly found out who they were!

What I heard on that recording changed my life forever. Instead of hearing dark, abstract, weird, or "old-timey" music—which is what most kids my age thought jazz was—I heard happy, joyful, high-energy, finger-poppin' music. And even though that concert had been recorded in 1953, it didn't sound old at all! From that day on, I was hooked. I had just started taking bass lessons at school, and I decided that I wanted to learn how to play jazz! After discovering "Dizzy" and "Bird," I soon learned about Miles Davis, John Coltrane, Duke Ellington, Count Basie, Louis Armstrong, Art Blakey, Sarah Vaughn, Billie Holiday, and many others.

Today, artists such as myself, Roy Hargrove, Nicholas Payton, Joshua Redman, Antonio Hart, Cyrus Chestnut, Gregory Hutchinson, Mark Whitfield, Jonny King, and many others have one thing in common: We are all very young, which goes to show you that this music is alive and well. There is such a fresh, vibrant spirit in the world of jazz, and there's no reason why anyone should not have a chance to discover this wonderful art form. Pay no attention to the images of jazz musicians you continually see in the movies and on television: weird, drugged-out, struggling, down-hearted artists. Just experience jazz for yourself! My friend and baaaaaad pianist Jonny King will help you.

Make no mistake, this music is for *everyone*! Black, white, young, and old. Jazz is not an exclusive, elite club. You can listen to your Snoop Doggy Dogg, your Pearl Jam, your Garth Brooks, and your Mozart, but add a little Ellington, Basie, or Coltrane to your life. I promise you will re-discover yourself!

—*Christian McBride*

INTRODUCTION
Getting Familiar

YEARS AGO I returned to my college dorm room, nearly coma-
tose from another insufferable Renaissance history class. I put
on *Relaxin' with the Miles Davis Quintet*, dropped the needle
on "I Could Write A Book," and lay down on our secondhand
sofa. Red Garland's eight-bar intro, Miles's muted statement of
the melody, John Coltrane's roaring solo—I was instantly trans-
ported away from lectures, exams, and crummy furniture, and
my head was bobbing with the pulse of Paul Chambers's bass
beat. Something about that record has always rescued me, no
matter where or from what.

My roommate barged into the room midway through Red's
solo, and I opened my eyes. He grabbed his baseball cap and
said to me, "So, is this number three or number four?" I shook
my head, not understanding. Mark, knowing full well that I
spent roughly half my nights playing piano in local jazz clubs,
continued, "You know, isn't jazz just, like, five or six songs that
you guys play over and over? This sounds like number three or
maybe four." He smirked as he left the room.

Flustered and annoyed, I reverently put on John Coltrane's
A Love Supreme, side two, first cut, "Pursuance," and turned up
the volume. This whole record is a monument to Coltrane's
spiritual rebirth and rediscovery, and I doubt there is a more

passionate, intense exploration of musical possibilities in recorded music. Elvin Jones begins with a thunderous, rumbling drum solo, then Trane, McCoy Tyner, and Jimmy Garrison charge in with the melody. McCoy is off and running over the entire range of the piano keyboard, and my heart starts to race. . . .

I was jarred out of my reverie when Andrew from across the hall charged into the room. "What the hell is going on in here? It sounds like someone's strangling a chicken." At that very moment, Trane was dwelling on a screeching high note, and I wondered how Andrew, or anyone, could *not* get it? Why was the music I love so opaque to many people?

As an upperclassman, I began to organize and perform in regular monthly concerts on that same college campus, featuring top young jazz artists from New York: Ralph Moore, Kenny Garrett, Steve Nelson, and many others. First, the closet jazzophiles came out. They knew the artists and the music, and I was glad for their support. The audience ranked high in enthusiasm, if low in numbers. But then more and more students started to show up. They came out of curiosity, boredom, by happenstance, or because they wanted something to eat at the student center where these concerts took place. It didn't matter why, just that they were there, and in numbers that shocked me.

Their initial curiosity soon became bona fide interest, and their interest began to translate into knowledge and familiarity and love. I started to run into some of these familiar faces at the local record stores, and they were buying Miles, Charlie Parker ("Bird"), Bill Evans, and Wynton Marsalis.

Now, well over a decade later, I see some of my newer friends and acquaintances going through the same process. They buy a few records, maybe read an article or see a movie like *Round Midnight*, and before you know it, they are hopelessly hooked.

It finally dawned on me. Jazz, even modern jazz, is not some arcane art form, reserved only for the cognoscenti. It can be accessible, even in its most abstract forms, and can speak instantly to and move listeners with the same force as any concerto or rock song. What jazz lacks is not inherent appeal but familiarity itself. People just have not heard as much jazz as they have Mozart or the Who. For whatever historical and perhaps racial reasons, jazz has never had the economic clout or mainstream support to become as ubiquitous as other music. While much of the typical music-loving public shies away from jazz because they think they don't "understand" it—a refrain I hear often—classical or "legit" musicians sometimes dismiss jazz as a "popular" music unworthy of serious study. Neither impression is justified. Jazz is great music, plain and simple. When it becomes even slightly familiar to people, it invariably wins them over.

Jazz can be immensely complicated and brooding. As often as it can sound happy or sweet or shy, it also can be abstract, remote, churning, even upsetting. Much of my favorite jazz is anything but pretty, in the standard sense. But that breadth of emotional expressiveness is part of why jazz is such great music. With a little preliminary interest and willingness to listen, anyone can understand and respond to jazz. It involves different sounds and instruments, and is based on a principle of improvisation that makes it less predictable and accessible to some neophytes. And as is the case with twentieth-century painting, for instance, a little knowledge and understanding of how jazz works will greatly enhance your appreciation of the art form and make you want to hear more.

The purpose of this book is to familiarize you with some of the core ideas and elements of jazz, to help you become comfortable with the acoustic bass, lengthy tenor saxophone solos, and improvisations that can take you to a million unanticipated places. You will be introduced to some exemplary recordings that illustrate many of the elements of jazz as they have evolved historically. This book is not a primer on jazz history—of which there are many—although the historical development of jazz and improvisation is a necessary part of any discussion of how this music operates. Nor is this book the equivalent of a music appreciation class where you memorize what is recognizable in jazz's twenty greatest hits.

What Jazz Is is an invitation to see how jazz works in simple terms and from the perspective of a working professional musician. You will get an insider's look at how musicians choose their set list; the way musicians base their solos on song forms and interact with one another during improvisation; and the continuity that links Duke Ellington, Thelonious Monk, and Sonny Rollins to the current batch of young musicians.

Don't get me wrong; jazz does not have to be an acquired taste. You can buy a jazz CD and become entranced right off the bat. I bought my first jazz record when I was nine years old, and I became a fan immediately. But if you take the time to learn the basics about jazz music and familiarize yourself with the players, you will enhance your listening experience immeasurably. Open your mind—and your ears—and begin the wonderful process of exploration.

PART I

JAZZ

BASICS

Francis Wolff/Mosaic Images

Thelonious Monk

Sonny Rollins Vol. 2 *session, Hackensack, New Jersey*
1957

Where's the Melody?

IT'S NINE O'CLOCK on a Thursday night, and you are midway down the steps leading into the Village Vanguard on Seventh Avenue South. The Vanguard, you have heard, is *the* place to see live jazz, a club where many historic performances were recorded. You have heard live jazz only once or twice before, but definitely not in such an august setting. The poster outside confirms that Mr. X is playing with his quartet, composed of musicians whose names you don't recognize. But your friend, who purports to be an aficionado, has told you Mr. X is a living legend.

At the bottom of the steps you shell out fifteen bucks and are shepherded to a table off to the right. As you notice that the drums are kind of obscured by a pillar that inexplicably interrupts one half of the stage, the waitress informs you that there is a ten-dollar minimum and that you should order now. Famous or not, this club certainly does not look like much. Generic Formica tables, a nondescript bar in the back, and the smell of musty carpet and cigarette smoke. There are photographs on the walls of people you guess are former greats, but little else distinguishes the Vanguard from a barely furnished basement. Plus, how can it have a pillar in the middle of the stage?

The crowd suddenly hushes as four men sneak behind and

around the pillar and mount the stage, such as it is. One is clearly older and carries a tarnished tenor saxophone. You assume he's Mr. X. The pianist sits down, then you notice some disturbance around that portion of the drums that you can actually see as the drummer steps in. Finally, the last member of the band lifts his acoustic bass upright. It looks like a giant violin, an overgrown cello, and its master plucks a few notes that boom so low you hear more of a rumble than a pitch. X turns to the band and whispers, "One . . . two . . . one, two, uh, uh, uh," and the music begins.

Hey, you recognize the song! You can't remember the title or lyrics, but you have a CD of Frank Sinatra singing this song, and you love it, although this quartet seems to be playing it awfully fast. You triumphantly recall the title, "The Way You Look Tonight," and watch. Soon you are transfixed by X's fluid statement of the melody. Then a loud crack or pop from the drums silences the band for a millisecond, and X runs off about a zillion notes in the blink of an eye. Through some sort of telepathy, the pianist, bassist, and drummer knew exactly when to stop and exactly when to come back in. The interlude somehow seems to be both orchestrated and spontaneous, expected but unplanned.

X is now off and running. He plays high and low and, above all, fast, with remarkably little movement, other than the blur of his fingertips sliding over the keys of his saxophone. Piano, bass, and drums are still involved, but it is X who commands everyone's attention. He makes what seems to be occasional reference to the melody of "The Way You Look Tonight" but otherwise seems to be playing a different song, or songs. It sounds great, this barrage of notes and sounds, intense and electrifying, but after your momentary thrill of recognizing the song, you feel a little disoriented. Where's the melody? What's going on? The drummer is starting to play louder as X builds the intensity. The bassist is playing a steady stream of notes you can't exactly decipher, and the pianist jabs away at the keys in a way that seems to coordinate with what X is doing. Audience members are tapping their feet and fingers, but to a beat you are not sure you quite grasp.

X now appears done, even though the song isn't over, and the audience applauds. You join in, enthusiastic but a little jarred. Attention shifts to the pianist, who now begins his solo. You've practically forgotten they started out playing "The Way You Look Tonight" as he does on the piano something like what X did on the sax. These guys' technical command of their instruments is impressive. They can play fast and faster, and you don't know whether they've memorized what they're playing. If so, who wrote it? Is this improvisation? How does it work?

When the pianist is done, X assumes center stage again and begins another solo. Do they play more than one solo per song? But this time X's solo is very short, and the drums take over, unaccompanied. Then X and the drummer take turns, each playing fast in a sort of call-and-response pattern. They are trading, playing off of each other, and again the pianist and bassist know precisely when to join in with X and when to leave space for the drums. This stuff must be preplanned. Nobody could just make it up on the spot, could they?

All of a sudden, out of the blue, they are playing "The Way You Look Tonight" again. It just happened. They flowed seamlessly from the organized chaos that left you excited, if discombobulated, into the comfortingly familiar. The experience was incredible, but you're not sure you understand what just happened. Even if you could remember the lyrics, you certainly could not have sung along with this rendition of the song. The audience applauds wildly, and you join in, a little unsure about what you witnessed but thirsting to know more.

Jazz in Context

So, what happened at X's imaginary gig? Above all, improvisation happened. Improvisation sets jazz apart, defines it, makes it special, and gives jazz its unpredictability and excitement. Improvisation makes jazz a truly spontaneous art form and imbues it with the constant capacity for change and moment-by-moment metamorphosis. There is some improvisation in other American music; rock and blues guitarists do take solos, and some classical pieces call for brief improvised cadenzas. But improvisation is at best incidental to rock and legit music. It is, however, the heart and soul of jazz.

Music does not have to be totally predictable to be beautiful. But for the neophyte listener, the unpredictability that makes jazz uniquely spontaneous and compelling also makes it a little daunting and intimidating. You simply can't sing along with a live improvised solo, because the soloist is composing notes on the spot, as he or she plays them. "Where's the melody in jazz?" is a refrain I've heard often, and it betrays a kind of discomfort some people have with the music. But as you learn more about improvisation and other components of jazz, you'll become aware that there is plenty of melody in jazz, as well as harmony and rhythm.

What exactly is improvisation? In simple terms, improvisation is extemporaneous musical composition. The soloist literally composes the solo as he or she plays it, in every bit as real a way as Beethoven composed his sonatas and the Beatles composed "Eleanor Rigby." Spontaneous composition is anything but random, however. Some other kinds of music *are* based on randomness. For instance, aleatory music is governed entirely by chance. John Cage, an aleatory composer, will place a number of radios on a stage, turn them to different stations, and let the vagaries of what comes out of the boxes determine the sound of the "music."

Jazz operates very differently. When Mr. X and company took to the stage at the Vanguard, they reached a kind of musical understanding. They agreed on a song to play—"The Way You Look Tonight"—and chose a key, a tempo, and the appropriate swing beat for it. Then, within the structure of that song, each musician had unfettered freedom to express his own perspective on the music and his familiarity with the vocabulary of jazz as it has evolved over time. In a sense, each musician recomposed "The Way You Look Tonight." It's like going down a tortuous ski slope. The slope and its inevitable descent establish the course for the whole ride, but the twists and turns make each skier's run unique.

In many ways, the jazz performance you witnessed at the Vanguard reflects a level of organization and structure commensurate with the most thoroughly composed concerto. Mr. X and his quartet did not simply make up what they played out of whole cloth, without any reference or relation to what was happening on stage and what had been played historically. Jazz is all about context, both historical and immediate. There are three major ways in which context gives jazz its meaning and sense.

First, jazz improvisers start with and draw on a common, shared body of musical ideas and expressions that have evolved through the years, although individual artists reinterpret these musical concepts in their own voices. Virtually every jazz musician first learns to play by listening to records and live performances. But rather than slavishly imitating what previous improvisers have done, the jazz musician internalizes and redevelops those ideas into her own style and voice. She starts with the past but speaks into the future.

Second, individual jazz improvisations are usually based on an underlying song whose harmonic and rhythmic structure loosely dictates or guides what the soloists choose to play. That underlying structure is the organizing principle out of which the solo flows. Therefore, when Mr. X solos on "The Way You Look Tonight," he creates new melody lines, rhythms, and, to a lesser extent, harmonies based on the underlying form of that song. Drawing on the vocabulary of musical ideas he has learned by listening, he essentially writes a new song based on "The Way You Look Tonight."

Third, much of what the soloist creates is influenced by what is happening musically around him. In other words, Mr. X's solo reflects not only his sense of the language of jazz and the underlying song structure, but also what the pianist, bassist, and drummer are doing at that precise moment. Because jazz is a music of communication, where artists within one ensemble must constantly stay in touch, Mr. X listens and responds to what his band members are playing.

Now you are over the first hurdle: You understand, at least abstractly, that improvisation is both spontaneous and organized, a moment of instant inspiration but also a reflection of historical and musical context. Still, there are a lot of questions to be answered. How do musicians acquire the vocabulary of jazz, and does it limit what they play? How does one "base" a solo on something else? What exactly is the relationship between the song and the improvised solo? Can you, as a regular listener, hear how these various elements are linked? Absolutely. Stay tuned.

Jimmy Katz/Giant Steps

Chick Corea and Kenny Garrett

A Verve recording session, New York City
1995

The Language of Jazz

2

TRYING TO DESCRIBE how jazz musicians improvise is difficult, not because improvisation is a secret rite shrouded in mystery, but because it doesn't translate well into words. Experiencing an art form is always better than talking about it, and with music in particular, hearing it is better than reading descriptions of it. Still, there is plenty to talk about that will amplify your understanding of and appreciation for what you will hear when you listen to jazz.

We will discuss the process of improvisation in two ways: metaphorically and technically. We also will touch on some musical terms—on the assumption that most of you are nonmusicians—that are basic to the concepts of melody, harmony, and rhythm, and look at the relationship between the organizing principle of the underlying song and the solo it inspires. The metaphor will give you the flavor of improvisation and a frame of reference, while the technical explanation will flesh out your understanding.

Neither approach is meant to obscure the basic emotional power that fuels jazz. That power you will hear on your own; ultimately, it has little to do with structures, forms, or metaphors. You don't need to "understand" a blessed thing to appreciate jazz as much as the most seasoned expert. But some understanding of the process jazz musicians go through will elucidate how they give voice to those emotions. As with any kind of music, the more you understand, the more you'll be drawn in, and the more richly you will hear.

A Musical Conversation

Let's start with the metaphor. It's been lurking in much of what I already have said. Jazz is a language through which musicians communicate ideas, emotions, and images to each other and to listeners. When I sit down at the piano and improvise, I am speaking a language I have developed over the course of decades of playing and listening, a language I have inherited from the likes of Louis Armstrong, Charlie Parker, Miles Davis, and countless others. I have learned that language by absorbing what those greats have "said" through their instruments on the recordings I grew up listening to, and by "speaking" with the musicians I play with now.

Indeed, the way a jazz musician learns the language of the music very much resembles how an infant learns to speak. You aren't taught in a formal sense. First you listen, without much ability to speak, and start trying to make sense of what your parents are saying. After a while you say your first words by imitating the vocal sounds you've heard. Soon imitation gives way to real expression. Speaking is no longer a matter of simply repeating what your parents and others say, but of using words to express your own needs and ideas. The language, with its rules of grammar and expansive body of words and expressions, serves as the common ground of communication, but it is still just a tool through which we express our individual thoughts.

And like language, jazz has its own set of clichés, turns of phrase, and even famous quotations. Every jazz musician has played "licks," the stock material handed down from generation to generation. Usually, it is a great jazz luminary who originated the lick in a particularly burning solo; others who admired it rehashed and redeveloped the lick. Just as William Shakespeare coined expressions that we still use, Charlie

"Bird" Parker played lines that virtually every modern jazz saxophonist has quoted.

The continuity is amazing. I sometimes hear a rock and roll background sax player play a lick that Bird invented fifty years ago. Both saxophonists speak the same language. I see the same principle at work on the current jazz scene, where teenage pianists imitate the improvised lines of the ubiquitous (and fabulous) Mulgrew Miller, who is only forty years old. Sometimes, when you see musicians laughing or smiling at each other on the bandstand, one of them has just played a familiar lick or a quotation—maybe from a famous solo by Coleman Hawkins or something as silly as a nursery rhyme. Perhaps the soloist deliberately played a wrong note or reharmonized and seriously altered something otherwise familiar. It's all part of the language of jazz.

But does this language limit the options you have and the directions you can take as an improviser? No way. The basic language and its vocabulary are only the starting point for an improviser's imagination. Homer and Shakespeare and Dostoyevsky weren't limited by their languages. They took hold of the language they had been taught and created something unique and personal. Jazz musicians do the same, and the possibilities of expression remain endless.

Let's take the language metaphor one step farther. Once you have the ability to speak and to express your ideas, you don't simply ramble on in disconnected thought. At least not most of the time. Rather, you bring your expressive skills to bear on a topic of conversation or an anecdote or an idea you have. That topic is very much like the song you choose to improvise over. When Mr. X and company selected "The Way You Look Tonight," they chose a topic of musical conversation. The notes and rhythms they played to each other and to the audience all spring from and have reference to the subject of the underlying song.

And the way a typical jazz performance unfolds is a lot like the way a conversation progresses. Someone chooses a subject to discuss and takes the lead in expressing ideas and thoughts about that subject. She is soloing, "blowing" over the contours of that subject. Her fellow conversationalists comment intermittently with ideas and thoughts that the speaker has inspired and that will, in turn, inspire her. They are accompanying her ("comping," in the parlance of jazz) and making the conversation an interaction rather than a soliloquy. They'll soon get their turn to take the lead in the conversation through their own solos.

Jazz musicians invoke this language metaphor all the time. Sometimes, when younger musicians are starting to ramble, to lose their focus and content, the older musicians will admonish them to "tell a story." Be concise, be eloquent, think about what you want to say. Some soloists play a lot of notes—they're wordy. Some soloists are deliberate and cautious—they're pithy. Some tell multiple stories at the same time, while others string together a thread of ideas, each connected to the previous one. For every manner of talking—loud, soft, solemn, playful—there is an analogue in the language of jazz.

As a nonmusician listener, you don't have to learn the fine points of this language to understand it. Buy yourself some records—Duke, Miles, whoever strikes your fancy. Listen. The music's passion and logic will begin literally to speak to you. You'll start to hear jazz improvisation as a marvelous, impassioned conversation. You'll hear the players telling their stories, being eloquent or scattered, serious or funny. You'll become more attuned to the communicative quality of improvisation.

With the language metaphor as a backdrop, it's now time to tackle some of the concrete stuff. Most people have at least a basic sense of the elements that make up musical composition: melody, harmony, and rhythm. This understanding has nothing to do with reading music or even with playing an instrument. If you've listened to music just a little bit and sung an occasional melody to yourself, you can easily grasp how improvisation works. I'll give you my spin on these elements from a jazz musician's perspective.

Melody is what you sing. When you hum a tune, or think of a song, you are first and foremost hearing melody. Jazz musicians improvise melodies, only we have different names for them. We play "licks" and "lines" and "ideas," and we "blow" over the song we have chosen to interpret. After Mr. X stated the melody of "The Way You Look Tonight," all those notes he improvised were his interpretations of new melodies.

Harmony is the underlying quality that defines what you sing. From the jazz musician's perspective, harmony has to do with what most people call chords, the grouping of notes played simultaneously. Play the notes C, E, and G together, and you have a happy-sounding C-major chord. Move the second note down from E to E-flat, the black note on a piano keyboard just below E, and you have changed it to an austere C-minor chord. If melody defines the singable line that lingers in your head, chords and harmony invest the notes of that melody with a certain mood and texture. Jazz musicians, and piano players in particular, love to take familiar melodies and reharmonize them, change the expected harmonies to something less orthodox. Check out the way Art Tatum or Herbie Hancock can completely alter an otherwise familiar melody by changing the chord structures.

Rhythm is an all-encompassing notion for jazz musicians, and it may be the most important element. Mulgrew Miller once suggested to me that you can play almost anything when you solo, any melody or harmony, and if you play it with *rhythmic* conviction, it will sound right. I agree. The general notion of rhythm in jazz embraces a number of specific concepts.

One of these concepts is tempo, the relative speed at which you play a song. The faster the song, the shorter each beat is. Ballads are slow. Medium-tempo tunes are "in the pocket." Superfast songs are "burning" or "upstairs."

Rhythm also has to do with the length and placement of notes in relation to one another. Take a string of notes as an inchoate melody line, and you can play those notes in different rhythms, some longer than others, some farther apart or closer together. Think about how "Mary Had a Little Lamb" would sound if you made the "little lamb" part last twice as long. You can phrase that simple melody endless ways rhythmically.

A piece's rhythm is also informed by its time signature. The typical time signature is four/four, that is, four beats to each measure, the rhythmic subdivisions that make up a song's structure. (A waltz has three beats to the measure.) Jazz musicians have experimented with all kinds of crazy time signatures, sometimes superimposing one over another.

Rhythm can also refer to the "groove" or "feel" of a piece. When I write a song and rehearse it for the first time, the drummer is apt to ask me what kind of rhythmic groove or feel I hear for that song. Do I want a swing beat or an Afro-Cuban feel? Maybe a Brazilian bossa-nova beat or a loose "Elviny" kind of feel reminiscent of the style of Elvin Jones? Do I want the bass player to "walk" or play a more broken feel? We'll get into these terms in later chapters.

Finally, rhythm takes in the elusive but essential concept of "swing." If I've led you to believe that improvisation is the single defining element of jazz, I haven't given you the whole picture. To be able to swing—*that's* the goal of every jazz musician. You can improvise the most brilliant, incisive melodies, but if they don't swing, you're not really playing jazz. You've probably heard Duke Ellington's famous song "It Don't Mean a Thing If It Ain't Got That Swing." It may sound a little hokey, yet it's true. We'll discuss the swing factor at length in the next chapter; for the time being, just think of it as that "spang-a-lang" drumbeat that everyone considers the definitive jazz sound.

Let's apply these concepts to a tune Mr. X might have played at the Vanguard. Take a look at the "lead sheet" on page 15, which spells out the melody, chords, and song form for one of Thelonious Monk's many great compositions, "We See." Monk was a genius, plain and simple, and much of that genius lay in writing almost childlike melodies that somehow manage to be endlessly hip and inspiring to blow over. Some of his best tunes are so sophisticated largely because they are so deceptively simple.

Whereas written music for classical performers indicates every note

We See

Lead Sheet

Medium up swing

Thelonious Monk

and rhythm the instrumentalist is supposed to play, a jazz lead sheet is, as you can see, a much more spartan road map. The performer, in a sense, has to fill in the musical blanks. So what does the lead sheet tell us? First, it spells out the notes and rhythms of the melody of "We See." You have to play these notes and rhythms at the start of the tune if you want to invoke Monk's composition. But there's plenty of room for interpretation. Mr. X. might, for instance, subtly alter the phrasing, changing the accents without departing too far from the basic rhythm, or he might dwell on a certain note or growl on a given phrase. His goal is to capture the spirit of the tune, rather than to play every single note the way Monk did. Like legit instrumentalists playing Mozart, the jazz musician interprets the melody of the tune and personalizes it, but has much more leeway.

On the lead sheet, the notes on the staffs of music define the melody; those symbols above the staff that read "G♭7" and "Cm7" and "F7" indicate the harmony of "We See." Those symbols represent the names of the chords of the tune, such as "C-minor seventh," a minor seventh chord in the key of C minor. When a piano player sees that symbol, he knows he has to play that chord. There are indeed many ways to play a C-minor seventh, many different voicings and subtle alterations you can make. But the essential tonality of the chord remains the same.

The chords of a tune collectively comprise the "chord changes" or simply the "changes" of that tune. Each chord has a special relationship to the one that preceded and the one that will follow it. Chord progressions or changes define the harmonic structure of a tune, and the way one chord flows into another is essential to what you hear. Standard tunes generally have pretty predictable chord changes, and even if I don't know a standard tune by George Gershwin or Rodgers and Hart, I can usually figure out those changes as I hear them by relying on my knowledge of typical changes. Many of the great jazz composers took these progressions much farther, however, and the Billy Strayhorns, Wayne Shorters, and Herbie Hancocks of the world came up with new chord progressions that interact in much less predictable ways, but which still retain an internal logic and beauty that make them sound natural.

Why should you care about something that sounds as technical as chord changes? Because to a large extent improvisation means playing over the changes, composing melodic phrases that coordinate with and reflect those changes. You don't have to be a musician to hear the relationship between the chords and the melodies that improvisers play over them. When a soloist is not playing the changes because she can't, you'll hear the awkwardness and the unwanted dissonance.

Melodies relate to chord changes in a number of ways. Every chord is composed of a collection of notes that define its sound. In order to qualify as a C-minor seventh, for example, the chord must contain a C, E-flat, G, and B-flat. So when you first learn to improvise, you tend to lean heavily on those four notes when playing that chord, because you know they will sound right.

But you soon learn that other notes work, that other scales fit the chord and increase your options. Innovators like Charlie Parker and John Coltrane took these principles many steps farther by incorporating the whole range of available notes into their solos, figuring out ways to make any string of notes fit rhythmically and harmonically into chord structures. They took the melodic choices and licks of their predecessors and redeveloped them into their own musical ideas.

Indeed, sooner or later, most improvisers realize that *any* note can work, depending on where you place it rhythmically and how you phrase it. Bird played all kinds of notes that in a technical sense conflicted with the chord structures over which he improvised, but he managed to place those notes in phrases that sound lyrical and melodic. A lot of modern improvisers—alto saxophonist Kenny Garrett, for instance—like to dwell on notes that most assuredly don't fit the underlying chord. I do the same thing. Those "wrong" notes create dissonances and tensions that can increase the drama of what you play, or give it a dark, idiosyncratic sound. The point is that improvised lines and notes are only "wrong" or dissonant, or "right" and pretty, in relation to the underlying chord they are played over. So when you improvise on a song with set chord changes—and most jazz songs and standards still have set changes—everything you play has meaning primarily in relation to the chord that underlies your choice of melody.

The final element that the lead sheet for "We See" reveals is the song's overall form or structure. Like all lead sheets, this one is divided into a certain number of subsections and musical measures, each of which represents a set number of beats. "We See" has a very traditional song form. It's in four/four time—that is, four beats to the measure—and is thirty-two bars long—that is, it contains thirty-two four-beat measures. (The first eight bars are repeated.) Each "chorus," as we like to call them, is thirty-two bars of the specified chords. Traditional song forms, which still underlie much of even the most modern jazz, tend for whatever reasons of historical accident to fall into multiples of four or eight.

The thirty-two-bar form, which Cole Porter, George Gershwin, and Thelonious Monk all used, is often broken down into an AABA form. That means that there are four eight-bar segments: two basically identical A sections, followed by a B section (or bridge), followed by a repeat of the A section. The AABA song form is an absolute standard in American music, and when you're on the bandstand, and you have to learn on the spot a song that everyone else up there knows, it helps a lot if someone informs you that the tune is AABA.

Song forms help organize improvisation both for the player and the listener. When Mr. X improvises over "We See," he plays new melodies over the chords *and* form of that tune. In other words, he'll play any number of AABA, thirty-two-bar choruses, improvising over the chord changes as they are laid out in Monk's song structure. That's what it means to play "over" a tune.

That's pretty much it for the technical stuff. I'm not trying to teach you to play, nor do I suggest that you commit these concepts to memory and try to discern them in the next live jazz performance you see. The point is only that improvisation, as free and extemporaneous as it is, has a kind of logic and context that links the elements of a jazz performance and makes it coherent. The melodies, rhythms, chord changes, and song forms we have been talking about are the ground rules. We improvise in relation to and within those rules, sometimes observing them scrupulously, sometimes stretching them, and sometimes violating them gleefully to make a point.

Those rules, to return to the metaphor, are the grammar and topic of our musical conversation. We build on what was said before, and each of us puts our own unique spin on the subject at hand. Ultimately, we speak the language of jazz.

Jimmy Katz/Giant Steps

Elvin Jones

A James Williams recording session, New York City
1994

Spang-A-Lang—
A Feel and a Groove

3

"Man, they are seriously *in there.*"
"Totally in the pocket."
"They're tippin' now, boy."
"Some serious spang-a-lang. Titi-boom!"
"God, but they're swinging! What a groove."

ANY CONCEPT THAT inspires that many euphemisms and that much excitement has to be important. The swing factor. Just like improvisation itself—and perhaps to an even greater degree—the notion of swing defines jazz and gives it its essential flavor and sound. Indeed, even if its practitioners had contributed nothing to twentieth-century music other than the swing beat, jazz would still occupy an enormous space in the musical landscape of the world.

Having said that, I'm afraid that I'm rather limited in what I can do on paper that will communicate what it means to swing. First of all, I'm still trying to figure it out myself. As fundamental as swinging is to any jazz musician, it's also something we work on our whole lives. You can always swing a little harder, be a little more deeply ensconced in the pocket. You have to approach the notion of swing with a great deal of humility and with the knowledge that it has been refined by great players for the better part of a century.

Second, swing is a difficult concept to put into words. Improvisation can be likened to language, and we can at least break it down into its constituent parts: chord changes, song forms, and the like. Swing doesn't even afford us those kinds of opportunities, however, because there is literally nothing technical about it, no music theory to discuss or lead sheets to dissect. It might be possible to transcribe what some very swinging drummers and other instrumentalists have played and try to discern what made those licks and phrases groove so hard, but that would disserve both those soloists and our efforts to grasp the swing factor.

Ultimately, swing is about a rhythmic feel, something as elusive as a groove. It is the ultimate "you'll know it when you hear it" kind of commodity. If you see a group that is really swinging hard, the energy of that swing will communicate itself to you, propelling the band and the audience forward. In fact, one of the reasons I believe jazz is much more accessible than most people realize is that there is something intuitively, instinctively communicative about swing.

In its most elemental sense, swing refers to a certain kind of beat, a certain kind of rhythmic feel that is unique to jazz. The "spang-a-lang" rhythm a jazz drummer plays on his cymbal is the building block for swing. The beat literally goes "spang, spang-a-lang, spang-a-lang, spang-a-lang," or "daa, da-da daa, da-da daa, da-da daa." Few jazz drummers actually adhere to that exact rhythm measure after measure, but the principle of spang-a-lang underlies much of what they do.

Add to this rhythm a strong emphasis on two and four, and we're getting closer to defining a swing beat. The majority of jazz songs are still in four/four time, four beats to every measure. Jazz drummers have historically emphasized the second and fourth beats of those measures to enhance the feeling of swing. Now drummers from other genres— funk, for example—do the same. The pattern goes something like this: one, TWO, three, FOUR. The key is that jazz musicians emphasize the offbeats of two and four, rather than the downbeats of one and three.

One of the first steps in your conversion to a hipster, in fact, will be to learn to snap to this rhythm. If you can hear the "one, two, three, four" of each measure of a jazz performance, try to snap your fingers or tap your feet on the offbeats, on two and four. At first it may feel a little unnatural stressing offbeats, but you'll soon hear that emphasizing the offbeats fits in perfectly, coordinates with the spang-a-lang rhythm smoothly and even locks everything into place. You'll also notice how the musicians on the CD or up on stage are doing the same thing. The drummer may, for instance, be sounding his hi-hat—the two concave cymbals that clang together when the drummer steps on a foot pedal—on two and four. The bassist may be accenting those beats as well.

So does spang-a-lang plus the offbeats equal swing? Not even close. They are merely a sampling of some of the rhythmic ideas we call swing beats. You can play them as faithfully as possible and still not be anywhere near swinging. Remember, swing is about a feel or a groove, and reading notes off a printed page will never add up to something so intangible. I have seen high school and college band directors struggle to get their students to play written-out lines with a "swing feel," but they invariably fail if those students haven't really listened to some good jazz. The feel of swing is as much a part of the language of jazz as are the licks and quotes and improvised lines we inherit by listening. You learn to swing by listening to Louis Armstrong or Miles Davis or Sonny Rollins or Milt Jackson. Sooner or later, it becomes natural and the only way you can imagine speaking the language of jazz.

Let's now expand our definition of swing a little bit. Jazz bands of course play many songs that don't fall properly under the spang-a-lang rubric. In addition to swing beats, as you'll learn in chapters to come, we play Afro-Cuban grooves, bossa novas, funk beats, shuffles, and New Orleans second-line beats. We play waltzes in three/four time, compositions in five/four or seven/four, and sometimes free pieces with no time signature at all. A drummer can't simply spang-a-lang his way through these different feels, but he can definitely swing on all of them. I recently saw drummer Idris Muhammad with pianist John Hicks's group. They were playing Hicks's "Naima's Love Song," a pretty, Latin-flavored piece. All I can say is, you can't swing much harder than Idris was grooving over that Latin beat he was playing, even though he wasn't exactly spang-a-langing. It's not the particular rhythm you play as much as the feel you bring to it.

Relaxed Intensity

Probably one of the best characterizations I've heard of what it means to swing came from the restless mind of Professor William Fielder of the Rutgers University Jazz Department. Jazz is most certainly not an academic pursuit, and it is my firm belief that jazz can't be taught but must be absorbed by listening. Still, Professor Fielder—"Profsky"—had a certain way of making clear to you what it was you were trying to achieve. I never went to Rutgers, but I was in several bands he directed and had the "privilege" of being bellowed at by him.

Profsky would stand in front of the piano, fist clenched and waving wildly in the air, and yell, "Come on!! You got to have that *lift!* I need to hear some more *lift!!*" You'd ratchet up the intensity in response, and he'd soon detect that you were getting increasingly tense, and gesture for the band to stop. "Relaxed intensity—that's what you need. Buoyancy. Lift. Intense but relaxed." A little hard to relax with a madman in your face, no doubt, but Profsky had the right idea.

When jazz is really swinging—whether it's a solo pianist, a quartet, or a big band—there is indeed an unmistakable feeling of buoyancy and lift. The underlying pulse of the tune—four beats to the measure if the song's in four/four—provides a kind of moving foundation, like the current of a river. Everything else, from the melody notes of a saxophone to the chords of a piano, floats on top of that current yet is also part of it, giving the whole performance the feeling of leaning forward, driving on inexorably. And while that movement is powerful and relentless, at its best, it is also supremely relaxed. As Profsky said, relaxed intensity is the key.

The feeling of lift built into swinging is great from both the listener's and the performer's perspective. If you are listening, you can sense the forward motion, the way the music literally propels itself onward. If you're part of the band, the feeling of swing locks the band together and lets everyone speak his or her piece in the context of the forward motion. As a pianist, I know that if the drummer is spang-a-langing with the right kind of intensity, and the bassist is locked into what the drums are doing, that hookup provides me with a solid foundation over which I can float. I can play in and out of the rhythms and chord changes, but the foundation of bass and drums and the pulse they provide make the whole performance hang together.

The capacious nature of the concept of swing is apparent in the incalculable number of ways jazz musicians accomplish that feel. A good illustration is the diversity of ways in which the great jazz drummers from the '50s and '60s—my own favorite period—swung. Give the same song at the same tempo to the most influential drummers, and all would have come up with radically different but uniquely expressive means of making the tune swing.

Philly Joe Jones, Miles Davis's drummer in the late '50s, was known for his "snap, crackle, pop," for the clean articulation and crackling fire of his swing beat. You can hear his legacy of crispness and clarity in young drummers of today like Kenny Washington and Greg Hutchinson. Art Blakey, who for four decades led different versions of his spectacular Jazz Messengers, was less like a smoldering fire than a volcano constantly erupting. His swing is less about precision and "pop"— although he was far from sloppy—and more about raw, untamed energy and soul. One of his most distinctive trademarks was a potent shuffle, an almost exaggerated emphasis on two and four, the offbeats, that could literally rock the house.

Elvin Jones, who helped define the then radical sound of John Coltrane's quartet in the early and middle '60s, sat astride a different kind of volcano. When people talk about an "Elviny" feel, they roughly mean a constant, heavy rumble with a triplet. In other words, each of the four beats of a typical four-bar measure might be broken down into three-beat triplets, around and through which Elvin would create his swirling rhythms. But Elvin's playing was so incredibly loose, his beat and phrasing so flexible, that the effect is that of a rumbling, rather than an erupting, volcano, breaking out in spurts and buoying the whole band up from his deep, low sounds.

During the same time period, Tony Williams was defining a different kind of approach to swing, equally loose but much splashier and jabbing. If Elvin took Art Blakey's volcano many steps farther, then Tony took Philly Joe's approach to a new level of snapping, crackling, and popping, slashing out crisp rhythms and counterposing different meters and beats against each other. Elvin's swing beat and cymbals sound nothing like Tony's, but they both are devastating swingers.

I don't mean to pigeonhole any of these drummers or to ignore the countless ways other artists put their own stamp on swing. My intention, rather, is to bring home the point that swing courses through the history of jazz and characterizes its essential rhythmic spirit. Jazz is a highly rhythmic music, and in some respects, melody and harmony can even take a backseat to rhythm at the most basic level. The continuity that makes Sidney Bechet from the '20s and Joshua Redman from the current scene part of the same musical tradition is in large part the rhythmic notion of swing. There are a million ways to swing, but at base all those ways share a certain unmistakable feel and groove. They all refer to and echo something about that spang-a-lang rhythm that makes music jazz.

PART II

THE KEY PLAYERS

AND THEIR

REPERTOIRE

Jimmy Katz/Giant Steps

Christian McBride

New York City
1996

The Rhythm Section

4

ONE OF THE first steps in figuring out jazz and appreciating how it works is understanding the individual and group roles of the various instrumentalists. As described in the previous chapters, jazz is a music of collaboration; although soloists are given their moments to shine, improvisation is a collective enterprise drawing on the contemporaneous imaginings of multiple musicians. At a recent gig, one intrigued but perplexed enthusiast asked me, "How do you all know what the others are playing? I mean, it's all happening *at the same time.* Don't you get in each other's way?" Well, sometimes, but usually not. The goal is to mesh collectively, and everybody has a personal and group role to play. The individual attributes of the key players and the nature of their respective roles are the subject of the next two chapters.

This chapter focuses on the "rhythm section," the heart of most jazz ensembles. The rhythm section traditionally refers to the piano-bass-drums combination that grounds most jazz groups, although certainly not all. That combination also comprises the classic "piano trio," of which there have been so many wonderful iterations, from Oscar Peterson to Ahmad Jamal to Cedar Walton. Guitar is also loosely defined as a rhythm section instrument and has been integral to other versions of the "piano trio," such as Nat King Cole's swinging drummerless trio of piano, guitar, and bass.

Why is the rhythm section so important? For one thing, these musicians play throughout the performance, both to accompany the other soloists and to state their own solos. Whereas a sax player, for instance, might remain silent after finishing a solo and might not reappear musically until the melody of the tune is played on the way out, the rhythm section usually plays continuously during the performance of a given piece. Sure, a pianist or drummer may drop out, "stroll," or "lay out" during all or sections of another player's solo, but you generally hear piano, bass, and drums all through the performance, either as accompaniment or as solos.

The foundation the rhythm section lays, a kind of carpet over which the others walk, is implicit in its name; the rhythm section defines the tempo, groove, and rhythmic feel of a performance. When the band leader "counts off" a tune—you might hear, "one, two, one-two-three-four"—the drummer, bassist, and pianist must lock into that tempo immediately and define it for the whole band. Similarly, if the leader decides that the piece will have a Latin groove, for example, the rhythm section must establish that groove, with the drummer and bassist playing the appropriate "clave" rhythm and the pianist adding the proper accents and phrasing to make the song sound right.

Beyond rhythm, which is the collective responsibility of all members of the rhythm section, the pianist and bassist (and/or guitarist) must establish the harmonic content of the tune. They must lay down the chord changes in the relevant song form, as discussed in chapter 2, so that the soloists can improvise over those changes. They will certainly improvise even in their accompaniment, with the pianist choosing different voicings for a given chord or occasionally even substituting harmonies, or the bassist walking different bass lines and breaking up the rhythms. However, the essential role of laying the harmonic groundwork remains the same, and everyone else in the band relies on the support of the rhythm section.

Indeed, no band can transcend its rhythm section. No matter how spectacular the soloist, he or she is necessarily held back or thrust forward by the support, inspiration, groove, and spirit of the accompanying rhythm section. Saxophonist John Coltrane, who undisputedly ranks as one of the most restlessly creative improvisers of all time, was so musically eloquent largely because he created in the environment established by his rhythm team of McCoy Tyner, Elvin Jones, and Jimmy Garrison. No matter how hip a trumpet player Miles Davis was, the unmistakable "vibe" of the classic Columbia recordings he made in the early and middle '60s is due as much to the fertile collaboration of his rhythm section—Herbie Hancock, Tony Williams, and Ron Carter—as to Miles's own mournful, idiosyncratic solo style.

The rhythm section is where it all starts, in other words. It makes everything work, from spang-a-lang, to chord changes, to the ultimate "vibe" of the music. Let's turn to the individual players.

The Acoustic Bass—Learning to Walk

What a misunderstood instrument the acoustic bass is. It is large and physically impressive, and booms with the lowest of sounds and greatest of rumbles. Yet it is also a fragile piece of wooden sculpture that resonates in the background of the musical consciousness of most listeners. The bassist typically stands toward the back of the stage, and, depending upon the acoustics of the environment, the instrument is often difficult to hear clearly in live performance and confounding to record with true fidelity. Still, good bass players are always working, the most in-demand cats on the scene, and you simply can't have a good band without a good bass player.

The physical makeup of the bass is a wonder. Take a violin, with all its delicacy and fine balancing of tensions and woods, and blow it up to the size of a small person. Then attach four fat and relatively inflexible strings made of steel or gut or steel wound around gut. Those strings are thick and difficult for the bassist to pluck, much less press down against the "neck" of the instrument to change the pitch of plucked notes. If we mere mortals try to play a few notes, both our hands hurt, and it is no wonder most bassists' fingers are thickly callused.

Bassists are constantly taking their instruments into the shop to have them fine-tuned (no pun intended) and to have the neck worked on or the bridge—that stiffener that holds the strings away from the body—adjusted. Sometimes more major repairs are needed, as in the case of Essiet Okun Essiet, a former bassist in Art Blakey's Jazz Messengers and Freddie Hubbard's Quintet. One day, just minutes before going on the road, Essiet set his bass out on his Brooklyn stoop so that he could run upstairs to grab his travel bag. The bass was in a flight case, which is about the size of a coffin and is built like an armored tank. He got back downstairs just in time to see the crusher of the garbage truck that had mistakenly scooped up the massive instrument, pulverizing both the case and its contents. The loss was devastating to Essiet, for the bass often represents the better part of the net worth of its owner.

So what is it about, this big wooden box? It's about time (in the musical, rather than metaphysical, sense), rhythm, harmony, and groove. The bass is literally the pulse of any jazz band, and whether you hear it closely or just feel its presence, it is as crucial to the sound of jazz as any other single element.

Unlike classical bassists, jazz bass players spend most of their time plucking rather than bowing notes. The bowed bass does have an important role in jazz, and performers from Slam Stewart to Paul Chambers to Christian McBride have all taken wonderful bowed solos. But first and foremost, a bassist must learn to "walk" by plucking with the right feel and the right notes. "Walking" denotes that steady, one-note-per-beat "thump thump" that emanates from the bass. If the song is in four/four time with the standard four beats per measure, a walking bass generally plays one note on each beat. In other words, the "one, two, three, four" time signature of the song translates into "thump, thump, thump, thump" on the bass. As we'll discuss in a moment, bassists do a lot more than simply walk their way through a tune, and even the simplest walking is usually broken up by the performer; but as a preliminary matter, walking is at the heart of how most bassists play. Built into this deceptively simple walking thump is a whole world of subtlety and musical sophistication.

First, there is the rhythmic feel that the bassist provides. Here again, the lingo abounds. Bassists who are robust rhythmic walkers have a "big beat" or a "strong pulse." The really swinging ones have a "serious hump." "Beat," "pulse," and "hump" represent efforts to put into words the percussive and rhythmic "boom boom" a bassist can provide for fellow band members.

"Pulse" may be the most accurate, because the bassist's walking is indeed like the heartbeat of the band. Often, in a comfortable acoustic environment, you can literally feel the bassist walking, feel the powerful attack and vibration of each beat as it buoys the solos. "Boom, boom, boom" or "thump, thump, thump" has been essential to jazz recordings and performances from Count Basie to Joe Henderson.

The great bassists—all bassists, for that matter—have different senses and theories of where they place the beat even when they are simply walking in four/four time. That notion might seem to make no sense at first, because a basic "four to the floor" walking pattern would suggest a plucked note on every beat. Yet some bassists like to play on top of the beat, while others play in the middle of or behind the beat. The tempo remains the same, and if you wrote out what each played, the transcription would be identical.

Still, as a matter of feel, some bassists, like Ron Carter, seem almost to anticipate the next beat by a nanosecond, just enough to make a barely discernible difference in the feel of the tune. He's not rushing or picking up the tempo, but rather providing a kind of forward motion within the prescribed tempo. His mastery of that subtle rhythmic approach creates a level of swing that thousands try to imitate by playing "on top."

By contrast, Ray Brown, a big-toned master of the blues, seems to like to do the opposite at certain tempos, to "lay back" behind the beat and strike his walked notes almost after the beat has occurred. He manages to keep a blues in the pocket like no one else. Both Ron Carter and Ray Brown have world-class "time"—the ability to keep a tempo steady throughout a piece—and their different approaches both work magnificently and swing hard.

Christian McBride, perhaps the busiest new bassist on the scene, told me how confused he was about this whole issue when he got to New York. He'd heard that in the Big Apple, most of the cats like everything to be on top, to have that edge provided by anticipating and nearly pushing the beat forward. That approach did not come naturally to Christian, but he adjusted his playing to fit his expectations. Drummer Kenny Washington, a die-hard traditionalist and self-proclaimed "jazz maniac," set Christian straight; don't worry about pushing the beat, just play good time and try to lock in with the drummer. Chris relaxed into his considerable natural groove and beat that falls somewhere in the middle between "on top" and "laying back." Since he's a first-call bassist, most people obviously don't have a problem with where he's landed. Good bass players adjust their beat to accommodate the situation at hand.

Closely tied to the whole notion of a bassist's beat is the bassist's "sound." When speaking admiringly or disapprovingly of a bass player, other musicians nearly always advert to his or her sound or tone, the relative resonance and power of each plucked note. The variety of possible sounds is staggering, and the one a bassist chooses—or has to live with, given his own limitations—radically affects his groove and overall contribution to a group.

The bassist's sound is determined in part by the quality and size of the instrument as well as the type of strings used. While cheap basses are made of plywood, expensive ones are constructed of exotic woods, and each kind of wood will produce a different kind of resonance. Basses vary in size, with the three/four bass dominating the jazz scene, although large seven/eight instruments and various smaller models are also used. Bass players will typically use either gut strings or steel strings. Gut strings, which are a rough-textured translucent beige, have a sharp, percussive attack and "thump" but less ability to sustain a note than steel strings, which ring longer. The debate over gut versus steel strings still rages in the bass community, with traditionalists opting for gut and more modern players using steel. Some use a combination of the two: steel wound around gut.

Finally, amplification seriously affects bass sound for better or worse. Some purists simply refuse to play amplified if the circumstances permit, reasoning that the resonance of the wood is the most natural sound. Others install a "pickup" on their instruments so that they can plug directly into an amplifier and access all the volume they want. Others compromise, eschewing the pickup but playing into a microphone positioned in front of their "F holes," those two squiggly line openings carved into the front of the bass.

One way to nose your way through the history of the bass is to compare sounds. The great bebop bassists had superstrong thumps born of gut strings and forceful plucking. Charles Mingus had a potent attack that drove the large, raucous ensembles he fronted. Ray Brown, whether with the Oscar Peterson Trio or his own groups, has a sprawling, deep sound thick with the blues. Ron Carter, who is largely responsible for defining what modern bass playing should sound like, has always had a smooth attack where each note is clearly articulated but sustains into the note that follows. The next time you play a CD, listen closely to the sound of the bass and how it enriches (or disrupts) the ensemble sound.

Now that we've covered the intertwined elements of rhythm and sound, let's take a look at the notes bassists play. Those notes are crucial, the harmonic underpinnings of the whole performance. It's not enough for a bassist to have a strong pulse and big sound; he or she must also play good "changes" and "lines." The bass player is at the bottom, quite literally, of the harmonic pile and must lay down the basic notes with which all the other chords and melodies in the performance have to coordinate. The bassist must keep the song's structure together and help spell out the chord changes for the other soloists.

Typically, the bassist will emphasize to some extent the "roots" of those chords, the bottom notes that give the chords their names. The root of a C-minor seventh chord, for example, is the note C. However, the bassist does much more than play roots, of course, and if you focus on the bass, you will hear melodies in the bass lines akin to those horn players improvise. Indeed, one of Ron Carter's greatest achievements is to play bass lines that are devastatingly hip harmonically but that also stand alone as beautiful, logical melodies.

From the harmonic and rhythmic standpoints, the bassist must be constantly responsive to the soloist's maneuverings. If, for example, the pianist begins to play around with a tune's chords, to substitute one change for another or alter the basic tonalities of a given chord, the bassist must adjust his notes to accommodate the shift immediately. As a soloist, you really appreciate the bassist with big ears, because you then have the freedom and support to explore new, unanticipated musical territory.

Now, for purposes of breaking down the discussion, we have neatly oversimplified the bassist's role by focusing on walking with the right rhythms and harmonies as an accompanist. The fact of the matter is, bassists rarely walk straight through a performance. Sometimes they will start a song with a "two feel" for the "head," or melody, of the song, emphasizing the first and third beat, and then break into walking for the solos. They can create a certain kind of drama this way, where the walking feels like a kind of release into unbounded swing. More generally, bassists, particularly modern ones, break up their bass lines rhythmically and depart regularly from a straight "four to the floor." They might simply add triplets or rhythmic accents to their lines, or more ambitiously play broken rhythms throughout a performance.

The rhythmic freedom of "modern" bass playing actually started a long time ago. As early as the '50s, Charles Mingus was willing to break away from a walked line into a freer rhythm. During the free jazz experimentation of alto saxophonist Ornette Coleman in the late '50s and early '60s, Charlie Haden perfected a kind of strumming, drone effect. Around the same time, Scott LaFaro, the virtuoso bassist of Bill Evans's piano trio, was constantly improvising adventurous rhythms and harmonies, melodically soloing simultaneously with the drums and the piano. Ron Carter and drummer Tony Williams in Miles's legendary band of the '60s changed tempos and imposed all kinds of cross- and opposed rhythms to the underlying pulse. But in all this experimentation, the principle remains the same as in walking: providing a rhythmic and harmonic foundation for the entire performance.

Finally, the bassist not only is in many senses the ultimate accompanist and ensemble player, but also is a soloist in his or her own right. Check out Paul Chambers's or Oscar Pettiford's various recorded solos, and you'll hear extraordinary improvisation in the bebop vein. Go hear pianist Tommy Flanagan's trio, and if George Mraz is playing bass, you'll hear an improviser with the fluidity and melodic sensibility of the great horn players. The bass is often in the background or the underground, but it can sing on its own, even as it makes the entire band swing hard.

The Magnetism of Drums

For whatever reason, drums have an intrinsic physical magnetism. I have been around drummers and their sets most of my life, and when the gig or rehearsal is over and everyone is packing up to go home, one of the other band members always manages to sit at the drums and hammer away for a while, however unmusically. Maybe the draw is rhythm itself, which feels like the most innate of musical elements, or perhaps it's the primal allure of banging on large resonant cylinders with sticks. Maybe it's just fun to produce all that volume and think you are making music by hitting things.

Whatever the precise etiology of drum appeal, the syndrome is clearly rooted in rhythm. Pianist Mulgrew Miller once shared with me his self-described "two-cent philosophy" that everything—music, traffic, adversity, heartbeats—marches to a rhythm, and that music captures that sense of rhythmic regularity. Rhythm does indeed seem to come first to most people. Tapping your feet or snapping your fingers is an expression of rhythmic purpose and excitement, and little kids tend to bang out rhythms before they do anything else "musical."

The drum kit is the quintessential rhythmic instrument and, along with the bass, is the rhythmic engine that drives the entire jazz ensemble. Drummers can't play chords, so they have no harmonic responsibility as such. Drummers don't deal in singable melodies either, although they do tune their instruments very carefully to cover a range of pitches from deep booms to high shots. Still, unless you're a real maniac, you don't hum drum solos, and the drums remain exclusively a rhythmic instrument.

Now, percussion of course plays a huge role in other musics. Rock and funk bands are fueled by their drummers, and classical music often incorporates highly technical percussion parts. But it is jazz that put drums on the map, or perhaps vice versa. The drum kit as it appears today developed out of the growing needs and wants of jazz drummers from the '20s to the present. The drums were quite literally made for jazz. And in this writer's humble opinion, jazz drummers have taken percussion to a different level, experimenting with every kind of groove, tempo, and combination of rhythms imaginable.

One of the best ways to get acquainted with the drums and start hearing what they are all about is to have a rudimentary understanding of the physical components of the typical jazz drum kit. Surprisingly, for all the stuff they play, jazz drummers generally use relatively modest sets compared with the multitiered behemoths favored by some rock drummers. Some jazz drummers even seem to delight in minimalism, in paring down their kits to the bare essentials to make the point that one cymbal or snare drum can be the vehicle for unbounded expression.

The "hi-hat" is a crucial piece in the drum kit. It is composed of a vertical rod at the top of which are two cymbals positioned horizontally with their concave sides facing each other. At the bottom of the rod is a foot pedal, which when pressed causes the two cymbals to clang together. When jazz drummers step on the hi-hat pedal, the two cymbals create that distinctive "chit chit" sound so essential to defining the pulse of a tune. Opening and closing the cymbals in different ways produces different effects. If, for instance, the cymbals are clanged together and then slightly separated, the cymbal overtones will continue to ring out. The hi-hat cymbals are also sometimes played like other cymbals by striking them with drumsticks.

The hi-hat has a defining role in the swing beat. Traditionally, the hi-hat "chit chits" on two and four, that is, the second and fourth beats of a four-beat measure. Those are the same offbeats that hipsters snap to, and simply accenting two and four with the hi-hat itself creates a feeling of swing. More modern drummers have, of course, freed up the hi-hat dramatically, playing it on all four beats or no beats or irregular beats. Drummers Jack DeJohnette and Billy Hart are masters of ever-changing hi-hat rhythms and textures. Next time you are at a club, watch the hi-hat and how the drummer's left foot controls a whole range of rhythms and sounds. Usually, there will be some two and four in there, and a good way to learn the swing feel is to try to key in to that emphasis and snap along.

The drummer's other foot operates the bass drum, the large, deep-sounding tub that sits on its side. The bass drum is sounded by stepping on its foot pedal, which activates a large felt-covered mallet that pounds the center of the drum. Bass drums, like hi-hats, can define the pulse and tempo of a tune. Traditionally, drummers played "four to the floor," pounding out a bass drum stroke on each beat like the bass player. The big-band drummers did this all the time, and I used to watch Art Blakey powering one of his shuffle beats with an incessant bass drum. Now drummers take many more liberties with the bass drum, using it as another means of accenting and layering rhythmic textures. Check out the wild array of rhythms Tony Williams created on the bass drum with his right foot.

That takes care of the drummer's feet; what about his hands? There are a series of drums and cymbals at his disposal. Sitting on a stand right in front of the drummer's midsection is the snare drum, positioned horizontally so that it can be struck with sticks using both hands. The snare has two basic sounds: When the snare mechanism is engaged, the sharp "chhh" sound associated with marching beats is heard; when it is turned off, the snare simply sounds like a higher-pitched hollow drum. Drummers, especially when playing swing beats, keep the snare engaged most of the time.

The snare provides the perfect percussive accompaniment. While a soloist is playing, the drummer comments and responds on the snare. The hi-hat may be chitting away, and the cymbals "spang-a-langing," but the snare pokes through with a sharp rhythmic commentary akin to a pianist's "comping" with chords. Drummers like Art Taylor ("A. T.") and Philly Joe Jones had a real percussive "thwack" to their snare sounds. Elvin Jones's snare keeps up more of a chatter with a triplet feel. Drummers jab away on the snare on offbeats, in between beats, and while repeating short patterns of beats, all to urge the soloists on and drive the performance as a whole.

Surrounding the snare are the "toms," usually in the form of one or two "floor toms" that stand upright and a regular tom or two held by a stand similar to that which holds the snare. Tom is a fitting name, because these drums resound in a distinctive "tom tom" sound somewhere between the deep boom of the bass drum and the sharper, higher-pitched snare. The addition of this midlevel sound means that the drummer has at his disposal a continuous range of pitches from low to high. Somewhat like the snare, these drums help accent and comment on the rhythmic performance of the soloing improvisers.

Finally, we arrive at the cymbals, whose sound may be the most conspicuous element in a jazz drummer's playing. Broadly speaking, there are two ways to use these metal disks, as "ride cymbals" and as "crash cymbals." The first is for "riding," keeping time and spelling out the pulse and feel of the tune. Riding is pretty much akin to spang-a-langing where a standard swing beat is involved. The ride cymbal defines the beat that the rest of the band uses as a frame of reference. If you watch closely during a gig, you'll probably notice the drummer favoring one cymbal over the others as a ride through-out the night.

The "crash," by contrast, is not conceptually tied to keeping the tempo and groove of the tune going, but rather accents certain beats with a crashing kind of sound. In other words, while the drummer's right hand may be spelling out a steady swing beat on the ride cymbal—"da, da-da dum, da-da dum" or something like that—both hands might periodically comment on the crash, maybe to announce the beginning of a new musical section or respond to the soloist's energy.

A drummer's cymbal beat is typically his signature, and seasoned jazz listeners can recognize a drummer simply by hearing a few measures of the ride cymbal. The great drummers, from Papa Joe Jones to Jimmy Cobb, Philly Joe Jones, Roy Haynes, and Tony Williams, all have a distinctive touch on their cymbals and a special way of spelling out a swing beat. Joe Chambers, still active, became identified in the '60s with a certain clarity and light openness in his cymbal beat, while Art Blakey during the same period placed his stamp on recordings with the sheer power and force of his cymbal beat. Without a strong cymbal beat, a drummer with tons of "chops"—a buzzword for technical virtuosity—is useless to a jazz band.

While we typically picture drummers with sticks in their hands, they also use "brushes." As the name suggests, brushes are made of metal or plastic bristles projecting from a handle akin to the back end of a drumstick. They can be swept across the snare or cymbal for a distinctive "ssshhhhh" sound that can be maintained continuously. The sibilance of the brushes helps provide a swishy backdrop for ballads, which rely less on a relentless spang-a-lang and more on mood and texture.

But that same swishy sound can fuel a ferocious swing beat as well. The sweeping is integrated with a kind of slapping on the snare, and the result is a whole different sort of rhythmic accompaniment. Swinging brushes and piano trios are inexorably linked in the jazz tradition. Buy an Oscar Peterson record featuring Ed Thigpen on drums, and you'll be treated to some world-class sweeping and grooving.

Hi-hats, snares, toms, bass drum, crash and rides, drumsticks and brushes—with all these resources, the drummer has a huge palette of sounds and flavors on which to draw both as an accompanist and as a soloist. Watching a skilled drummer is like a lesson in limb independence; each foot pounds out different rhythms while both hands glide over cymbals and drums faster than the human eye can see. And yet, despite the wealth of sounds that can be produced, the drummer's role remains a fundamentally simple, if protean, one.

The drummer is first and foremost an essential timekeeper for the band, establishing and maintaining the tempo and groove of a tune along with the bassist. It is the drummer who provides the rest of the band with a fast samba, or a medium swing groove "in the pocket." At the same time, the drummer is also a constant improviser, changing the rhythmic colors and textures of a tune in response to the band and the soloists. Every sound you hear is in some sense colored by what the drums have to say.

Let's now return to the Vanguard, where Mr. X and his group are playing "The Way You Look Tonight," and focus on the drummer's performance. The drummer starts out playing the "head" of that tune along with the band in relatively straight fashion, spelling out the tune's tempo and essential feel with the ride and accenting the highlights of the melody line with the crash or snare. Then, at the end of the head, the drummer pounds out a one-note "break," giving Mr. X and his sax perhaps two bars of silence to introduce the first solo.

During the course of the sax solo, the drummer will adjust his playing so he's headed in the same direction as the soloist. At first, he uses simple riding and sparse accompaniment on the snare, but then as the soloist builds in intensity, he starts to layer the rhythms with various patterns, cross-rhythms, and "polyrhythms." Watch how the drummer "drops bombs," explosive accents with the bass drum, snare, and toms, and shifts direction in sync with the soloist. The best drummers create their own kind of excitement within the melodies and ideas the soloist is developing.

Then the drummer takes the lead with his own solo, building from a quiet exploration of certain rudimentary rhythms to a thunderous barrage of sounds, rhythms, and percussive effects. (Drummers themselves are, like the rest of us, victims of drum appeal.) Next the drummer "trades fours" or "trades eights" with the soloists. In a typical thirty-two-bar song form, for instance, musical phrases can be divided into four- or eight-bar segments, and the soloist and drummer can take turns playing during these phrases, alternating every four or eight bars. Next time you see a drummer trading with a saxophonist or pianist, watch the call and response that develops. It's like a musical conversation between melody and rhythm.

Finally, after the band returns to the melody of "The Way You Look Tonight," the drummer ends the performance with a dramatic flourish, cued by Mr. X, on the crash cymbal. As keeper of the rhythmic flame and all-important swing beat, the drummer appropriately has the clamorous last word.

Everyone's a Piano Player

While musicians tend to gravitate to the drums at the end of the gig to make a little noise, most jazz players are actually reasonably decent pianists. Trumpeter Terence Blanchard, bassist Ray Brown, and saxophonist Eddie Harris all play excellent piano, and I once heard a trio tape of saxophonist Joshua Redman that I mistook for a demo of one of the up-and-coming pianists at the Berklee College of Music in Boston. The piano simply has it all in terms of melody, harmony, and rhythm, and virtually anyone trying to improvise must learn his or her way around the eighty-eight keys, conceptually if not technically. Most jazz composers create at the piano as well, even if their main instrument is a saxophone or bass.

The piano is, of course, far more familiar to most people than an acoustic bass or a jazz drum set, but the qualities that make it *the* instrument every jazz musician must at some level play are often misunderstood. First of all, for all its lush chords and romanticism, the piano is in many senses a *percussion* instrument, a vital part of the *rhythm* section. When you play a note on the piano, you activate a mechanism whereby a felt-covered hammer strikes a metal string stretched under incredible tension, not unlike the striking of a drum, although we pianists hope to evoke a little more finesse and beauty than "hammering" would suggest. Still, when you listen to the rhythm section, remember that the piano's role is a vitally rhythmic one.

Add to that percussive quality a harmonic breadth unmatched by any other instrument. With ten fingers, a pianist can literally play an infinite number of chords ranging from two-note combinations to full-bodied voicings using most, if not all, digits. The range of pitches on the keyboard, from notes so low their pitch is tough to discern to notes way above those the human voice can attain, multiplies the already infinite number of chord voicings at a pianist's disposal. Everyone in the band relies on the pianist to play those chords properly, to spell out the tune's changes and ground the soloist's wanderings. We all compose at the piano for much the same reason: to hear the harmonies we create to underlie the melodies we devise.

Finally, the huge expanse of the piano keyboard gives it the greatest melodic range of any instrument in the band. A tenor sax player is, for example, limited to a range of notes that fall somewhere in the middle of the piano keyboard, while the bass covers the lower registers. A pianist improvising melodies can choose from any of these registers and more, although she is likely to favor one area of the keyboard more than others. The point is simply that the piano can go to more melodic places than any other instrument. Indeed, the piano's only limitation is that it cannot "bend" a note, alter the pitch slightly upward or downward, the way a horn player or bassist can. The pianist pretty much has to stick to the pitches tuned on the instrument.

As a member of an ensemble, the jazz pianist brings all these features to bear on the whole performance. Until she solos, the pianist's key role is to "comp" behind the soloist's improvisations. Comping—a bastardization of the word "accompanying"—is a rare art indeed, one I've been working on all my life, and the reality is that if you're a good comper, you'll get the gig. Comping involves playing the tune's chord changes in a way that both supports and responds to the soloist. When Mr. X is blowing over a standard tune, he wants the pianist to spell out the chord changes of that tune clearly, but he also wants the pianist to pick up on the solo's rhythmic, melodic, and harmonic nuances.

Take my word for it, comping is no walk through the park, and while most pianists have a sort of automatic pilot mode of stock rhythms and chord voicings to play, the best compers are always listening and reacting. First, you must key in to the rhythms that are evolving. Maybe the drummer has started a repeating rhythmic pattern on the snare, or the soloist is continually landing on a certain beat or leaving a lot of space between phrases. You must hear those patterns or phrases and play rhythms on the piano that coordinate with them as they evolve.

While you're focusing on being rhythmically supportive, you must also attend to the harmonies involved. Are you making clear where everybody is in the tune's chord structure? Are you adjusting the chord changes to fit the harmonic chances the soloist is taking? Are you catching the bass player's chord substitutions, if not this chorus then the next time around (assuming that the bassist decides to play it the same way for the next chorus)? If the trumpeter is playing up high, are you choosing chords in an appropriate register of the piano to mesh with the tone of the horn?

Some compers are even genuinely melodic, although of course it is the soloist whose melodies take precedence. Herbie Hancock, for instance, tends to fit little melodies into the spaces left by soloists. When he was a member of Miles Davis's quintet and backed up two of the most eloquently spare soloists of all time—Miles and Wayne Shorter—Herbie meandered around their solos, blending small melodies into the whole musical weave.

In reality, the business of comping is both easier and tougher than it sounds. To just get by, I can simply sit down at the piano and comp chords that I know fit the tune's changes and that I think are swinging rhythmically. Any reasonably skilled jazz pianist can pull off such a performance. But comping becomes an art when it is truly responsive to the ensemble sound, when the elements of rhythm and harmony and melody blend seamlessly into the group performance. Some of my favorite compers, from Wynton Kelly to Herbie Hancock to Kenny Barron, are always responding, always commenting on what is happening in the group as a whole, and the impact they have is neither hidden nor inescapably subtle. Watch and listen to the great pianist compers, and you'll see and sense the constant interplay between the soloist, the band, and the pianist's comping.

What happens when the piano solos? Who comps for the pianist? The pianist's left hand takes over. While the right hand improvises melodies in much the same fashion as a horn player, for instance, the left hand comps chords and rhythms that support and complement those melodies. In other words, what a comping pianist does for a soloist he is backing up, the pianist's left hand does for his right hand during the piano solo. Next time you see a pianist in a typical jazz rhythm section, check out the interplay between the pianist's hands as well as that between the rhythms and harmonies spelled out by his left hand and the support the bassist and drummer provide. This quilt of sounds and textures blends into the group sound of the "piano trio," a term synonymous with "rhythm section" when it functions as an independent unit.

Some pianists have very active left hands that either provide powerful rhythmic backdrops for right-handed melodies, or double in octaves what the right hand plays, or even state independent contrapuntal melodies. A booming "take no prisoners" chord in the left hand is a signature of McCoy Tyner's percussive solo style, and Phineas Newborn's trademark was the lightning-fast runs he could play in parallel octaves with both hands. Other pianists have a more spartan approach. Keith Jarrett's left hand, capable of nearly orchestral density, sometimes drops out completely on his "standards" albums to let the right hand speak alone. Red Garland would punctuate his lucid right-hand melodies with a regular pattern of left-hand chords on the "and of two and four," that is, chords struck immediately after the second and fourth beats of each measure. The possibilities are endless.

Of course, the right hand is not limited to linear, one-note-at-a-time runs by any stretch of the imagination. Some pianists are indeed oriented toward single-note melodies. Bud Powell played bebop lines with his right hand akin to the melodies Charlie Parker spun out on the alto saxophone. Other pianists tend to play more chordally. Bill Evans,

Red Garland, George Shearing, Oscar Peterson, and others—all capable of magnificent single-note lines—are also masters of "blocked chords," melodies spelled out in thick chords. For Red Garland, those chords tended to involve octaves in the right hand, whereas for Bill Evans, the chords were denser and richer harmonically.

Until now, we have envisioned the pianist as part of an ensemble, matching his soloing and comping to the group dynamic that surrounds him. The piano, nevertheless, unlike any other instrument in jazz, also has a magnificent solo tradition. Even during the course of a typical small-group performance, bandleaders will often direct everyone to leave the stage to permit the pianist to play a song completely unaccompanied. On the many occasions when I saw Art Blakey and the explosive Jazz Messengers, he always gave the pianist an opportunity to shine on his own.

From the discussion in this section, it should be clear why the piano is the ideal solo instrument. Beyond the expansive melodic and harmonic resources available to the pianist, he has the unique ability to comp for himself with the left hand. "Stride" piano, an early solo style that still manages to find its way into the vocabularies of even the most modern of pianists, replaces bass and drums with the pianist's left hand. The left hand generally plays a bass note and a corresponding chord on each alternating pair of beats. "One, two, three, four" becomes "note, CHORD, note, CHORD" in the left hand, freeing up the right hand to solo as if the entire rhythm section were there. A variation of straight stride was "boogie-woogie," where the left hand plays a relentless repeated blues bass figure to keep the rhythms moving.

Stride is a seventy-year-old style that originated with pianists like James P. Johnson and Fats Waller. But it is also integral to more modern players from Thelonious Monk to Oscar Peterson to Mulgrew Miller. I tend to stride during much of my solo playing, because it provides such a strong rhythmic foundation over which to improvise. The way you stride generally mirrors your personality as a pianist. Teddy Wilson, who became known to the jazz world playing with Billie Holiday and Benny Goodman, had a gentle stride in his left hand reflective of his overall elegance as a pianist. One of the most harmonically and technically gifted pianists of all time in any genre of music, Art Tatum was capable of rapid-fire stride with sprawling chords. Classical virtuoso Vladimir Horowitz is said to have followed the unassuming Tatum around to get a glimpse of the impossible things he pulled off at the piano.

But stride is only one facet of the solo tradition. Unrestricted by the musical proclivities of other band members, a solo pianist has unlimited freedom to experiment with rhythms and harmonies and melodies. He can play "rubato," that is, with no clear time signature or feel, or substitute chords or alter melodies. Tatum was a master of re-harmonizing the most familiar standards extemporaneously. Bill Evans had a passionate and romantic way of rethinking standard tunes and reinventing them with lush harmonies and phrasing. Monk's idio-syncratic and jagged compositional style shines through his simplest solo excursions. When you watch a pianist play solo, you begin to see a range of capabilities that may not be noticeable during an ensemble performance.

The trio tradition parallels the solo tradition. The typical trio is, of course, the rhythm section standing alone as the band itself, although other instrumentation is possible. Two of the greatest trios of all time, Nat King Cole's and one iteration of Oscar Peterson's, involved piano, bass, and guitar instead of drums. But the typical trio is the rhythm section, and virtually every great pianist recorded in the standard trio format at one time or another. My own record collection contains trio material by Duke Ellington, Teddy Wilson, Bud Powell, Thelonious Monk, Wynton Kelly, Hampton Hawes, Oscar Peterson, Bill Evans, Her-bie Hancock, McCoy Tyner, Cedar Walton, Chick Corea, Keith Jarrett, Kenny Barron, and countless others. For sheer bluesy swing, it's tough to beat Oscar Peterson's trio with Ray Brown on bass. For rhythmic and harmonic fluidity, I can turn to the pathbreaking Bill Evans Trio or Keith Jarrett's collaborations with bassist Gary Peacock and drummer Jack DeJohnette. For great arrangements of both originals and standards and a deep groove, Cedar Walton's trio always satisfies.

In some ways, the best way to get into jazz is to watch the pianist.

You'll get a sense of percussion and rhythm, in combination with melody and harmony. You'll glimpse the essence of group improvisation and see how nonsoloing players support and comp for the lead instrument. In the interplay between right and left hands, you'll begin to understand how harmonies and chord changes underlie melodic improvisation. The piano is itself a microcosm of what jazz is all about. Once you get a sense of what the piano player is doing, everything else will fall into place.

Francis Wolff/Mosaic Images

John Coltrane and Lee Morgan

Coltrane's Blue Train *session, Hackensack, New Jersey*
1957

The Front Line
(and Others in Between)

5

IT'S SOMETIME IN the mid-'80s, and I am about to hear Art Blakey's Jazz Messengers for the first time. The club is Mikell's, a now-defunct jazz bar on the Upper West Side, and, although I have grown up obsessively listening to the Messengers on LP, I have never seen them live. Led by the indomitable Blakey and his drums, the Messengers have been around since the '50s, and it's tough to decide which was my favorite incarnation. The '50s group with Lou Donaldson and Clifford Brown? Early '60s with Lee Morgan and Wayne Shorter on the front line? What about a few years after that with Freddie Hubbard and Curtis Fuller joining Wayne on the front line? The group with Wynton Marsalis in the early '80s? The Messengers' alumni roster reads like a Who's Who of horn players.

Back at the club, I've heard that Blakey, known as "Buhaina" or "Bu," has a serious new horn section, with young lions Terence Blanchard (trumpet), Donald Harrison (alto sax), and Billy Pierce (tenor sax) fronting the band. Six guys in suits—Blakey about forty to fifty years older than the rest—mount the stage, and the rhythm section begins with a shuffling introduction. It's Wayne Shorter's "One by One," first recorded at the fabled Birdland in 1963. I'm hearing some legendary stuff by the guy who made it famous. Bluesy and incisive, the horns burst in with the melody, and I'm in heaven. The front line of two saxophones and trumpet blends magnificently, spelling out the harmonies of Wayne's arrangement with a few '80s alterations. Their sheer power and percussive "pop" is amazing. These guys sound as huge as a big band, but with the agility and freedom of a smaller ensemble. They simply couldn't be tighter.

Blakey's horn section has always exemplified what the front line of a jazz band does best. The rhythm section may comp throughout the performance, but it's the front line you notice first as it states the melody of the tune and usually begins the soloing. What you'll go home singing is what the front line played. I saw the Messengers many times after that first baptism, even played a few tunes with them on occasion when I "sat in," and each time I was blown away by the cool power of that front line. Blakey would simply make the players crackle—and cuss them out, I'm told, if they didn't. Who's up there on the front line? Details to follow.

The Saxophone — Jazz's Signature Instrument

For many casual music listeners, the saxophone is *the* signature instrument in jazz. Saxophones haven't really made their mark in other genres the way they have in jazz. Sure, rock bands often feature background sax parts, and there are indeed lengthy and wonderful classical compositions written for saxophone. But, like the drums, the saxophone evolved as a jazz instrument, its growth paralleling that of the music itself.

People tend to stereotype the saxophone. I've often heard the sax described as "sultry" or "sexy" sounding, and easy-listening radio stations feature "contemporary music" where the sax wails away in tones befitting B-grade thriller soundtracks. The reality is, however, that the sax has a range of tonal variations unmatched by any other instrument in the jazz ensemble. Saxophones can certainly sound "sexy," but they can also be harsh, growling, and even jarring. They can whisper or shriek, breathe warmth or spit fire, and a quick listen to John Coltrane's 1965 album, *Transition*, will disabuse anyone of the misimpression that the saxophone is limited to that canned sound you heard during the credits of *L.A. Law*.

All saxophones create sound when the instrumentalist causes a thin "reed" made of shaved bamboo to vibrate by blowing air into the mouthpiece. Saxophonists are always messing around with their reeds, soaking them before a performance and changing them after unsatisfying solos. I cannot remember a single gig with Billy Pierce, the aforementioned Jazz Messenger, when he didn't scowl after his first or second solo, shake his head, and change his reed. Then there's the mouthpiece, another object of obsession for sax players. "Why does this guy use such a large mouthpiece?" "How does he get air through that mouthpiece?" It all sounds like gibberish to the rest of the cats on the bandstand, but the size of your mouthpiece must be important, or sax players wouldn't talk about it so much.

The saxophonist changes pitches by pressing down keys, the little round buttons lining the sides of the instrument. While your mouth controls the intensity and tone of the notes, your fingers determine the pitches and lines you play. If you watch a video of John Coltrane, you'll hear an almost overwhelming torrent of notes, but you'll barely see his body move. The intensity is all focused on the saxophonist's mouth and fingers.

At a typical jazz concert, you are likely to encounter the soprano, the baritone, the alto, and the tenor—each of which sounds radically different. Let's begin by looking at the soprano sax.

The soprano saxophone, which has the highest pitch, is a narrow and straight horn without the curved bell characteristic of the other saxophones. The soprano has roughly the dimensions of a clarinet, and it is very difficult to play in tune. With some notable exceptions—Steve Lacy and Dave Liebman, for instance—few sax players are primarily soprano players, but rather double on the soprano as an alternative to their main "ax," a tenor or alto. Great players from Trane and Wayne Shorter to Branford Marsalis all recorded on soprano, even though they are best known as tenor saxophonists. The soprano is a bewitching instrument, with an almost Middle Eastern, snake-charmer kind of sound.

The other "second-tier" saxophone is the baritone, not so much because it isn't a great instrument, but because you don't hear it as much. The baritone is a large, curving, low-pitched horn with a characteristically growling sound. Pepper Adams was a great hard-bop "bari" player, who swung with the force and imagination of his compatriots on tenor and alto. Gerry Mulligan, a West Coast arranger and bari player, smoothed out the instrument and coaxed a prettier and softer sound out of it. The baritone sax also contributes mightily to the saxophone sections of some of the legendary big bands. Check out Harry Carney's wonderful contributions as the bedrock of Duke Ellington's sax section.

Between the soprano and the baritone sax lie the two most visible instruments in the reed family and maybe in all of jazz, the alto and the tenor. The alto saxophone evokes one name in all jazz musicians' minds: Charlie Parker, a.k.a. "Bird." As noted earlier, Bird's influence is probably as pervasive as that of any twentieth-century musician. He effectively invented modern jazz, spearheading the transition from the swing era and big bands of the '30s and '40s to "bebop," the demarcation point for all modernists. Songs and clubs—"Ornithology" (a song) and Birdland (a club), for instance—are named after him, and not only alto saxophonists, but also tenor players and pianists and bassists and virtually anyone who plays improvisatory jazz, will start with Bird. You would be hard-pressed to find any giant who cast an equivalent spell over an entire art form, and he did it all with his alto.

A curved horn, the alto is the next size down from the soprano and covers a middle range of pitches just below the soprano's and above the tenor's. The distinguished lineage of the alto starts before Bird with greats like Johnny Hodges, Duke Ellington's remarkable sideman, and the still-active Benny Carter. Hodges had a big, enveloping tone and passionate vibrato that defined the sound for many of Duke's anthems, such as "I Got It Bad and That Ain't Good." As an elder statesman, Carter continues to record wonderful music, swinging as hard and as joyfully as he did decades ago.

In the '40s, Bird built on the sound and phrasing of Hodges and others to create a new vocabulary. He was of course panned at first for playing so many notes, and "wrong" ones at that. His language was highly linear and technical, and his lines veered away from simply spelling out the basic tones of the chords. Like Hodges, Bird had a huge, pretty sound, but his concept was much more intricate and his articulation devilishly precise. Now musicians had to deal with the much more sophisticated language of bebop, which involved faster tempos—*much faster*—and irregular, highly syncopated phrasing. The notes were different too. Virtually every note was now fair game for every chord, for even though Bird always played "inside" the changes, he had a gift for playing "wrong" notes in the right place, with the right accents and phrasing. I'm still not sure that there is anything more "modern" in American music than Bird and bop, examples of which we'll hear in chapter 7. It's not weird, just supremely sophisticated and urbane.

Where do you go after someone with such a giant influence has hit the scene? The alto thrived. Julian "Cannonball" Adderley, a huge bear of a man whose nickname was a mispronunciation of the word "cannibal," was for many the consummate alto player. He first made his mark as a member of Miles Davis's classic sextet in the late '50s and then went on to a stellar career as a leader. Cannonball may simply have had the biggest sound of all time. And while he shared Bird's ferocious phrasing and awesome technical facility, he put a bluesy spin on virtually everything he played. If Bird was the greatest innovator on the horn, Cannonball may be the most fun to hear. He literally breathed soul and in fact incorporated a strong gospel element into his music with hits like "Mercy, Mercy, Mercy" and "Jive Samba."

Around the same time, in the late '50s and '60s, Ornette Coleman took the alto in a completely different direction. Ornette, too, was influenced by Bird, but he was avant-garde from the beginning. Ornette was the father of "free jazz," where the musicians dispense with chord changes and time signatures and sometimes even any kind of tonal center or key. Now the soloist had no song structure to refer to, no chords to suggest what to play or conventional four/four carpet over which to walk. In Ornette's hands, improvisation reached a kind of purified state, where more and more of the organizing but limiting factors of form, chord structure, and even pitch fell by the wayside. And yet what you hear is not chaos but some of the most spiritually gripping explorations ever recorded. We'll hear some Ornette in chapter 11.

The current scene still boasts some remarkable alto players. I have "sides"—that is, records—from the late '60s featuring Gary Bartz, but I have equally exciting ones of Bartz in the '90s. Phil Woods, an heir apparent of sorts for Cannonball, still tours the world, and Charles Mc-Phearson carries the Bird torch. Younger players abound: Bobby Watson, Kenny Garrett, Jesse Davis, Greg Osby, Steve Wilson, and a host of others. I have been fortunate to play with many of these artists. They all feel the influence of Hodges and Bird and Cannonball and Ornette, but they also have their own sounds and contributions to make. The alto's future seems in good hands.

For all of Bird's influence, the *tenor* saxophone occupies an equally giant place in the jazz universe. One compelling way to trace the history and growth of jazz is to follow the tenor players who epitomized the sound of each musical generation. If you check out what the tenor was about in 1942 or 1964 or three days ago, you'll probably get a good sense of where jazz itself has been. The tenor is that ubiquitous and that much of a force in this music.

Like the alto, the tenor, which covers the next range of pitches down from the alto, has evolved both in terms of the sounds musicians extract from the horn and the vocabulary of lines and phrases they create. Tenor players are *always* talking about their sound, their "tone." "Is it warm enough with this mouthpiece?" "Is the sound more breathy with this reed?" "He plays great, but I don't like his sound." "Some funny notes, but, boy, what a sound!"

The tenor players of the '20s through the '40s typically had a warm, breathy sound, open and dark, with a thick vibrato. Chu Berry, Ben Webster, Coleman Hawkins, and, later, Duke Ellington's magnificent sideman Paul Gonsalves defined the sound of several musical generations with the thick and palpable tone of their horns. Webster in particular had an incredible warmth and passion in his tone, even as he growled out the melody of a ballad. Hawkins ("Hawk"), for many the consummate tenor player of the swing era, brought to that sound a more modern vocabulary, presaging some of the harmonic risks and rhythmic idiosyncrasies that Bird would turn into bebop. Hawk's version of "Body and Soul" rates among the most famous in jazz history, and there probably isn't a tenor player alive who hasn't made reference to that solo in some way, shape, or form.

Some of the best prebop tenor players had names that somehow—not precisely, but by suggestion—tell you all you need to know. How else could Eddie "Lockjaw" Davis or someone with enough gumption to be named Illinois Jacquet sound, if not big and embracing and assertive? What about Ike Quebec? Gene Ammons was known as "Jug," and one of the great transitional, swing-to-bebop players was named Lucky Thompson. You probably had to have a measure of soul to walk around with names like those. The spirit was in the sound.

But there was at the same time another approach developing, much smoother and more mellifluous. Lester Young, known as "Prez" and identified by his trademark porkpie hat, had all the passion and groove of his gruffer compatriots, but in a much more debonair package. Some of my favorite sides are the collaborations among Prez, pianist Teddy Wilson, and "Lady Day," vocalist Billie Holiday. Here the passion is not about growling, or thick vibratos, but rather a smoldering purity of tone. The elegance of Prez's tenor sound, described to me by some older musicians as "silky," influenced generations to come. Stan Getz, a West Coast player who, among other things, popularized Brazilian bossa novas as jazz vehicles, was very much the Prez of the '50s through the '80s.

Oddly enough, with all this talent around, no tenor sax player in the late '40s and early '50s could make the leap to bebop. Coleman Hawkins, Lester Young, Don Byas, and others were all nudging their ways into a more modern vocabulary, but not with the immediate, take-no-prisoners intensity of Bird. It was only when Sonny Rollins arrived a few years later that the tenor had a larger-than-life spokesman to match what Bird was doing on alto.

Rollins, known as "Newk" and still very active, is a remarkable amalgam of old and new. He shares in the tenor's legacy of big, muscular, and warm sounds that fill rooms and can assault your ears. And although he is a fine composer, many of his most memorable recordings are of standard, sometimes even hokey, tunes that he revitalized and reimagined. No doubt even their composers did not expect that "Toot, Toot, Tootsie" and "I'm an Old Cowhand" could be made to swing so hard.

But for all his traditional sound and penchant for old standards, Rollins integrated into his style a fierce new rhythmic and linear twist. Like Bird, he began to play true bebop lines, where the whole scale was fair game and each chord suggested a broad new resource of altered notes. Perhaps more jarring was the fierce percussiveness of his phrasing. Each note had a power and impact that probably no other tenor player has ever equaled. And the lines and phrasing were so idiosyncratic, so unexpected and unpredictable, that it took critics a while to readjust their sense of how a jazz solo should evolve. If you check out some of Newk's trio recordings with drummers Elvin Jones or Pete LaRoca, you'll hear how he can drive the entire band rhythmically with the sheer power and momentum of his phrasing. In chapter 9, you'll hear a quirkier, more playful Newk with Thelonious Monk. Today, Newk still has a surreal bigness about him that tends to overshadow even the ablest of sidemen.

Rumor has it that in the late '50s, when Newk was the undisputed heavyweight champ of the tenor, he was forced to reevaluate his entire musical identity by the emergence of an even more radical and arresting voice on the instrument. After Newk left Miles's band, which had been, like Art Blakey's Jazz Messengers, a launching pad for so many key players, John Coltrane had taken over the tenor slot. Newk remained comfortable as the recognized champ until he heard Trane one night after a number of months on the road with Miles. Whether apocryphal or not, the story is that Newk simply quit playing publicly for a while after the revelation of Trane.

There are really several Tranes that you can hear on recordings. In the late '50s, as Miles's sideman, he was an incredible, restlessly inventive improviser whose lines spanned the full range of the horn, from its lowermost reaches to altissimo high notes, and stretched the harmonic limits of what everyone thought playing changes was about. The critical description was "sheets of sound"—layers and layers of notes and phrases and patterns. The sound itself was different, too. Trane was not speaking the wide breathy language of Coleman Hawkins or Sonny Rollins but had a newer and more incisive, almost metallic voice. To those unaccustomed to the sound, Trane was disturbing. Even as a teenager in the '70s, weaned on the sounds of Ben Webster and Chu Berry and Newk, I was thrown for a loop at first by Trane's riveting tone. It was too modern for me, even though it was recorded years before I was born!

Still, while Trane's sweeping approach with Miles was a revelation, Trane found his truly revolutionary voice in the '60s, as the leader of his own formidable quartet interpreting his own compositions. Backed by the thunderous trio of McCoy Tyner, Elvin Jones, and Jimmy Garrison, Trane set off in an entirely different direction, on a spiritual pilgrimage. The names of his records during this decade are revealing: A *Love Supreme* (1964), *Crescent* (1964), *Transition* (1965). Much of the music was what theoreticians call "modal," that is, based on scales and "modes" rather than standard chord changes. That description belies the depth of Trane's exploration, however, because no scale or rhythm or groove could hope to contain Trane's passion.

Trane was, in a sense, the next logical step after Bird. Bird had revolutionized playing changes by picking apart the harmonies and rhythms and vastly expanding the palette of acceptable notes improvisers could incorporate. Trane took another route by exploring what could be said over one chord or one scale or rhythm. Most of the tunes on *Transition* are based on only a simple collection of notes, but Trane teases every possible sound and phrase out of that grouping. His technical facility was probably the greatest of any saxophonist to date, and within one solo, he might shift from a dark, simplified beauty, to a blistering flurry of notes, to a series of sweeping near shrieks. Trane took the music to a new level of emotional intensity.

Trane has indeed proved to be an impossible act to follow, and he left future generations of players scratching their heads about what was next. Of course, Newk and Trane were both surrounded by magnificent contemporaries, who, though less purely innovative, moved the music forward by simply playing so well. Flourishing in the wake of Newk, Dexter Gordon's massive sound and unparalleled ballad playing won many admirers, as did Hank Mobley—affectionately known as the "middleweight champion" of the tenor—who swung as hard as anybody as a member of the Jazz Messengers, Miles's band, and as the leader of his own groups.

After Trane, new innovators also flourished. Joe Henderson, who has currently been "rediscovered" (although he never went anywhere), is still one of the most imitated tenor voices ever. Joe, too, is a supremely idiosyncratic player, with twisting, spinning lines, an almost vocal phrasing, and a catalog of much-played compositions. In the early to middle '60s, his string of records on the Blue Note label defined "hard bop/ postbop," the idiom that evolved in the generation following Bird and Newk. By the late '60s and early '70s, Joe's tenor took on a harder edge, reflecting the radical experimentalism of the day. Records like *Power to the People* (1969) and *In Pursuit of Blackness* (1971) defined the idiom of a tough sophistication, a militant beauty. Now Joe's approach is quieter and more introspective. He continues to evolve.

During the same period, Wayne Shorter took Trane's scalar approach in yet a new direction. While a Jazz Messenger, Wayne featured a big, rough sound and broad rhythmic honk. But when he joined Miles's band in the mid-'60s—a band that many consider to be the greatest triumph in group improvisation ever—Wayne's approach became more cerebral and focused. He had Trane's passion and probing imagination, but in a more elusive, almost deliberately nebulous package. His lines would bubble up, as if from underwater, and then resubmerge. His harmonies were constantly on the edge, always pushing the boundaries of what the chord might suggest. As we'll see in chapters 6 and 9, Wayne is one of jazz's great composers, and his playing reflects a composer's logic and sense of form amid the controlled chaos of Miles's band. Wayne was also one of the first to experiment with fusion and electronic music and cofounded Weather Report, the first great fusion band.

Hawk, Newk, Trane, Dexter, Joe, and Wayne present a daunting legacy for any tenor player on the scene these days. And yet the instrument flourishes. Some of the most creative musicians can be found within the ranks of tenor sax players. Joe Lovano, Branford Marsalis, Ralph Moore, Joshua Redman, and a whole host of names you will be starting to hear—Mark Turner, Chris Potter, Javon Jackson, Seamus

Blake, and many others—are continuing to explore the potential of this great instrument. They continue to prove that, however spectacular the contributions of their predecessors, the tenor's resources will never be exhausted.

The Egomaniacal Trumpet Player

Among musicians, trumpet players are reputed to have the biggest egos. As the other musicians see it, they're the cockiest guys on the bandstand. They tend to "beaugard," try to take over every tune and every gig and musical situation. Of course, such sweeping generalizations couldn't possibly be true for all trumpet players, but the trumpeter's reputation might be justified to a certain extent. You probably have to be somewhat brash to think that you can lead a quintet or power a big band's brass section with a pint-sized horn with only three valves.

The trumpet, like the saxophone, may have realized its greatest potential in the context of jazz music. Notwithstanding some remarkable classical concerti for the instrument, jazz trumpeters have taken the trumpet farther and exploited its musical potential more fully than have trumpeters in any other genre. Wynton Marsalis, whose jazz and classical recordings have won unprecedented critical acclaim, chooses jazz as the more fertile stomping ground for the trumpet. Excellent in both idioms, Wynton insists that jazz affords the trumpeter greater freedom to create and explore.

The technique of playing the trumpet is bewildering to the rest of us. The horn is a small curved piece of brass (or other, more exotic metal finishes) with a mouthpiece the musician blows into and a "bell" that fans out from the horn and projects notes and sounds. The mouthpiece is a small metal cylinder into which the trumpeter must blow his tightened, pursed lips. You can always tell trumpeters by their mouths and lips, which always bear the signs of having been forced into the cone of the mouthpiece. Dizzy Gillespie had even more battle scars. In an effort to force more air through the horn, he puffed his cheeks to such an extent that he destroyed the membranes lining the inside of his cheeks, and his face would blow up like a balloon when he played. The trumpet is an extremely physically demanding instrument, and you can't lay off for more than a few days without seriously compromising your chops.

Once you get a full head of steam and force air into the horn to create tones, how do you determine the pitches of those tones? With just three valves that you press down with your fingers. By combining different amounts of air pressure, changing lip positions, and pressing down different combinations of the three valves, the trumpet is able to sound about three octaves' worth of pitches. Most people are fairly blown away by the prospect of trying to control dozens of different notes with barely perceptible changes in lip position and valve alterations. I played the trumpet briefly, and I can attest to what a chore it is to sound the notes properly, much less play them coherently, swinging all the time.

But just playing the notes is hardly what the jazz trumpet is all about. Like all jazz horn players, trumpeters start by developing a sound, a recognizable tone. The trumpet has a reputation for being "brassy"— assertive and forward—but that impression is belied by its amazing tonal range. Skilled trumpet players can coax an endless variety of sounds out of the horn. They can blow with a potent sonic impact that cuts through the ensemble sound, over the other horn players and above the rhythm section, but they can also communicate with great warmth, with breathy, seductive tones as engaging as any saxophone's.

Jon Faddis, Dizzy Gillespie's protégé, has a terrific punch to his notes that makes him a great lead trumpet player in a big-band horn section. Chet Baker on the West Coast and Art Farmer in the East, by contrast, made their marks with darker, mellower sounds. Hard-bop masters Clifford Brown and Freddie Hubbard magically combine the power of great big-band–style players with an inviting smoothness and warmth on both up-tempo burners and ballads.

Beyond the pure tone of an unadulterated note, the trumpeter has a huge arsenal of devices and what might be deemed "effects" that radically change the sound of a given note. First, there are a series of "mutes," metal, rubber, or plastic cups that are placed inside the bell of the horn or over its perimeter. The Miles Davis sound of the late '50s features the "harmon" mute, which replaces the standard trumpet tone with a pinched, almost whistling sound. Miles's unique and instantly identifiable harmon mute sound proves that the mute doesn't genericize the trumpet sound, but simply affords the instrumentalist another way of developing a personal tone. The "cup" mute offers a more closed-in, almost nasal signature, while the "plunger"—which resembles the rubber thing you use to clean a clogged drain—permits the trumpeter to create a "wah-wah" kind of wail by opening and closing the air passage out of the bell.

Apart from the mechanical implements deployed, trumpeters create a number of different effects with their lips and fingers. Lee Morgan was a master of the bluesy "smear," bending notes up or down from the expected pitches by pressing the valves down halfway. More modern players like Terence Blanchard similarly slide pitches and attacks in and out of the expected sounds to great effect. Because the sound of the trumpet is controlled directly by the mouth and lips, trumpeters can essentially vocalize their musical ideas directly. The language metaphor becomes particularly appropriate in the case of the trumpeter, who effectively speaks through the horn.

Like the saxophone, the trumpet is an emblem of jazz history, and the idiom's development can be traced through the evolution of the horn. Jazz's first great improviser, Louis Armstrong, was a trumpet player. Because he became somewhat of a popular icon, a rare jazz star who won recognition among the general public late in his career, Armstrong's artistic achievements are underappreciated by that same public. Make no mistake; Armstrong was a genius, an innovator on a par with any other in jazz history. He was improvising sophisticated lines over chord changes in the '20s, before anyone imagined how liberated improvisation could be. Armstrong had the powerful attack and pure tone associated with great technical mastery, but he added a sense of swing and spirit that basically put jazz on the map as a serious art form. He was one of the first artists to play changes, to translate basic harmonies into extemporaneous melodies and lines. He also virtually invented what it means to swing. There can be no greater innovation than having spawned an entire idiom.

Armstrong was of course not completely alone. The '30s also witnessed the tragic life of trumpeter-pianist Bix Beiderbecke, who had a most fertile musical mind. Beiderbecke never achieved Armstrong's recognition, but he too was a forward thinker already experimenting with modern harmonies at a time when most musicians were simply coming to terms with the concept of chord changes.

Post-Armstrong, the mantle passed to the great swing trumpeters of the big-band era, such as Roy Eldridge and Cootie Williams. Eldridge, known as "Little Jazz," inherited Armstrong's brassy sound and trademark vibrato and moved it into the more open harmonies of the swing era. Bebop was around the corner, and Little Jazz and others like him were paving the way for the great bop masters, Dizzy Gillespie and Miles Davis.

Diz was the Bird of the trumpet. All of a sudden, the horn was opened up to a seemingly unlimited array of notes and harmonies and expected to play blistering tempos and angular bebop lines that seemed impossible within the trumpet's supposed technical limitations. Dizzy ignored those limitations and made the trumpet-sax pairing in front of a rhythm section the prototypical jazz small group, the classic quintet that remains the most familiar instrumental combination in jazz today.

Dizzy's technical prowess was outrageous, and I have heard chops-laden trumpeters like Freddie Hubbard marvel at how "tricky" Dizzy could play. Even Dizzy's big band of the late '40s eschewed the confines of the typical big-band charts of the day in favor of the bebop approach. The entire band was expected to play those wickedly intricate bebop melodies as a unit, and damned if Dizzy didn't make his big band sound like an overgrown quintet featuring Diz and Bird. Even after the heyday of bebop, Dizzy continued to evolve, popularizing the Afro-Cuban rhythms that have become staples for modern jazz artists.

Bird and Diz often recorded with a young trumpeter named Miles, who was mastering the bebop idiom even as he struggled technically. Miles never could play with the facility or brashness of Dizzy and the other emerging bop trumpeters, like Fats Navarro and Red Rodney. But Bird and Diz saw something special in Miles, something unique about his feel, his dark and brooding tone and brilliant melodic imagination. Their nurturing of the young Miles presaged the greatest and most protean career in jazz history.

Miles Dewey Davis is something like the Picasso of jazz. His career spanned so many styles and so much experimentation that he might be deemed a master of virtually every style that emerged from the bop of the late '40s to the endless musical variety of the present. After participating in the birth and fruition of bop, Miles began to explore a more introspective sound in the '50s with his *Birth of the Cool* recordings in conjunction with arranger Gil Evans. Those tight and harmonically rich arrangements surrounded Miles's mournful, spare approach and represented a complete departure from the speed and ferocity of bebop. The recordings were indeed "cool," with all the reserved sophistication of a West Coast sound from which Miles would soon flee.

Later in the '50s, Miles formed his classic quintet/sextet groups with a roster of the best players: Hank Mobley, John Coltrane, Cannonball Adderley, Bill Evans, Wynton Kelly, Red Garland, Philly Joe Jones, Jimmy Cobb, and Paul Chambers. Those groups kept some of the slick polish of the Gil Evans period but added a new fire closer to bop and what was known in the '50s as "hard bop." There was nothing reserved about the way Trane and Cannonball played, or the bombs that Philly Joe dropped, but Miles was able to maintain his characteristic savoir faire in the midst of this harder-edged sound. And while the late-'50s bands played a repertoire of familiar standards—"Green Dolphin Street," "Bye Bye Blackbird," and the like—they also began to experiment with more modal composition like "So What." Those recordings may have been the launching pad for Trane's rocket flight into modal playing during the following decade.

As the '60s rolled around, Miles's playing became more experimental and jarring. Still spare and occasionally self-effacing, Miles developed a penchant for choosing the most startling of notes and leaving space where you expected to hear a flurry of notes. The bands of that decade were up to the task of matching Miles's quirkiness and mystery. The rhythm section of Herbie Hancock on piano, Ron Carter on bass, and the eruptive teenager Tony Williams on drums was one of the most flexible in jazz history. When Miles played bluesy, so did the rhythm section, but when Miles veered toward abstraction, they instantly tuned in to his hazy harmonies and rhythms.

The saxophonists were equally up to the task. George Coleman—in New York City he's called "Big George" these days—and avant-gardist Sam Rivers paved the way for Wayne Shorter, Miles's alter ego in harmonic and rhythmic experimentation. The band's repertoire retained familiar standards, but they were now played with wildly altered harmonies and shifting rhythms. "Autumn Leaves" would start out fast and then ease into a slower tempo and a radical, spontaneous reworking of the standard chord changes.

Moreover, Wayne and Herbie began writing for the band, contributing masterpieces like "Pinocchio," "Riot," "ESP," and "Capricorn." The harmonies were at once deeply complicated but also open-ended, with plenty of room for alterations and reharmonizations, and many of the best performances of the day were totally freed up from any conventional chord changes. Still, what made this band so special was that, amid all the freedom, the harmonic waywardness and rhythmic explosiveness, it swung *incredibly* hard. Even the darkest abstractions somehow swung powerfully in this band, maintaining continuity with the jazz tradition while tearing down its barriers.

Thirty years later, *New York Times* critic Peter Watrous identified that mid-'60s quintet as the purest expression of group improvisation that jazz has ever known. And yet Miles plunged ahead into new areas. By the late '60s, his band incorporated electric piano and funk rhythms, and Miles was spearheading another movement, fusion. He continued on that path through the '70s and '80s. The one constant was that scary intensity and moodiness, a darkness to his sound and note choice. Whatever genre he explored, or, to be precise, invented, Miles always contributed a dark passion and soul that links his '40s bop to his '80s funk.

Like Bird and Trane, Miles influenced virtually every subsequent artist on his instrument. The years following bop witnessed the careers of a number of exciting young players. Clifford Brown was blessed with a fat smooth tone, and a unique melodic genius and swing feel. His '50s band with drum great Max Roach and Sonny Rollins was in many senses the quintessential postbop quintet, defining what the next generation was supposed to sound like after the furious innovations of bebop. Brown's untimely death in his mid-twenties doubtless deprived jazz listeners of untold wonders on the trumpet.

Kenny Dorham continued the bop tradition into the '50s and '60s, and brought his composer's sense of form and logic and a sweet, mellow tone to his solos. The great Clark Terry, who is still active today, continued the bop tradition introduced by Dizzy. Along with fellow Messenger Donald Byrd, cocksure Lee Morgan charged into the '60s with a bluesy fire and a giant sound that fueled the Jazz Messengers' little big-band sound. One big fat note on the radio, and you know that it's Lee on trumpet.

Freddie Hubbard may have been the consummate trumpet player of the period. With a gorgeous round tone and incredibly smooth and assured sense of swing, Hubbard epitomized the fire and eclecticism of hard bop. He was at once a pure bebopper—check out his early dates as a leader, such as *Open Sesame*—as well as an exponent of the "new thing" of the '60s, participating in radical combinations with Ornette Coleman and Trane. By the '70s, he, too, was incorporating the electronic sounds of funk into his recordings. If you catch "Hub" today, you'll still see him swagger onto the stage and smile assuredly as he whips off lines other trumpeters could never dream of executing.

Sounding initially a lot like Hubbard in the mid-'60s, Woody Shaw took a different approach into the '70s and '80s. With a similar sense of swing and an incisive attack, Shaw perfected a whole new vocabulary on the trumpet. Like Trane on sax and McCoy Tyner on piano, Shaw played angular, sometimes dissonant lines that departed from the standard melodic fare of the trumpet. He also created oblique compositions and had an edge similar to that which Joe Henderson brought to his recordings of the late '60s and early '70s. Shaw's recorded output is remarkable for its innovation, yet it has not received the attention it deserves. Many of his records, particularly the almost angry sessions of the '70s, have never made it to CD and remain out of print. Those recordings, with their snarling intensity and intricate harmonies, nonetheless continue to influence countless younger players.

The '80s was the decade of Wynton Marsalis as far as the trumpet was concerned. A native of New Orleans, Wynton, known as "Skain," was a bona fide jazz star while still a teenager. He brought to jazz not only a formidable set of chops but also a newfound legitimacy. Decked out in the slickest of attire, Wynton carried the imprimatur of the classical community and yet chose jazz as the most expressive art form. Unlike so many of his predecessors, Wynton was the antithesis of the drug-abusing, tormented musician. He was articulate, dead serious, and for better or worse altered the public's perception of what jazz musicians were like.

In Wynton's career as both player and composer-arranger, he has looked both forward and backward for inspiration. When he formed his own band in the early '80s, featuring his brother Branford on saxophone, he defined a sound that still permeates the jazz scene: incredible technical proficiency, tight-knit labyrinthine arrangements, and a controlled wildness. Wynton's classic early records, such as *Think of One* and *Black Codes from the Underground,* feature these qualities, as well as a style of playing known as "burnout." Burnout tunes are essentially free, with few if any chords and maybe an underlying vamp in the form of a repeated bass line figure over which the soloist plays. But unlike the wavering spirituality of Ornette Coleman's free-jazz explorations in the '60s, burnout is deliberately tight and tricky, with cross- and polyrhythms imposed over each other in dizzying fashion.

As the '80s progressed, Wynton changed direction, looking to standard popular compositions, the works of Duke Ellington, and his own New Orleans heritage. His current repertoire, both as leader of his septet and as director of the Lincoln Center Jazz Orchestra, reflects his tendency to revisit the past as a source for fresh compositional material.

The current scene boasts an impressive roster of trumpeters. Tom Harrell has a carefully burnished tone and talent for endless melodic invention, and has been entertaining audiences for most of the last two decades. In addition to Wynton, the younger set includes Terence

Blanchard, Roy Hargrove, Nicholas Payton (also from New Orleans), Scott Wendholt, and a host of other gifted players.

Other Woodwinds

While the trumpet and saxophone are by far the most ubiquitous wind instruments in the typical jazz ensemble, there are a variety of other horns you might see at a gig. Many saxophonists, for instance, double on other woodwinds such as the clarinet and the flute. The clarinet was popularized as a staple of the swing era by big-band leaders like Benny Goodman and Artie Shaw but has not played a major role in modern jazz. Certain gifted avant-garde improvisers, such as Eric Dolphy and Sam Rivers, recorded some fairly radical music in the '60s on the bass clarinet, a deeper-pitched sibling of the more familiar "licorice stick." Moreover, a number of current reed players, such as Eddie Daniels and Ken Peplowski, continue to specialize in the clarinet and ensure its place in modern jazz.

The flute occupies a similar position. Tenor saxophonist James Moody, a still-active bebop master, is a wonderful flute player as well. Alto saxophonist James Spaulding, who appears as a sideman on numerous records by Wayne Shorter and Freddie Hubbard, also doubles on flute and continues to record on the instrument. But except for a handful of players, such as Hubert Laws, few jazz improvisers are exclusively flute players.

On the brass side of the spectrum, the trombone takes a close second place to the trumpet. Unlike the trumpet, whose pitches are controlled by pressing down valves, the trombone has a large U-shaped "slide" that moves back and forth to alter pitches. If the trumpet's technical demands are daunting, the trombone's seem impossible in the context of modern jazz. Trombonists Edward "Kid" Ory and Lawrence Brown were regular members of Louis Armstrong's and Duke Ellington's ensembles in the '20s and '30s, and a trombone section grounded virtually all of the big bands of the '30s and '40s, but the instrument seemed too cumbersome and technically limited to make the transition to bebop.

Nevertheless, J. J. Johnson proved that bop, with its breakneck tempos and angular melodies, could indeed be played on the trombone. Having played with Bird four decades ago, J. J. is still active as a bandleader and composer and remains the dominant presence on the instrument. His sound is big and smooth, and he plays with the grace and agility of a saxophonist.

In the hard-bop idiom, Curtis Fuller and Slide Hampton followed J. J.'s lead, as did West Coast players such as Carl Fontana and Frank Rosolino. Along with Freddie Hubbard and Wayne Shorter, Curtis Fuller was in one of the strongest Jazz Messengers groups ever and proved that trombone could cut it with the galvanic force of Blakey behind him. Slide Hampton, noted as both a performer and arranger, shares much of J. J.'s facility on the horn.

Grachan Moncur staked out trombone's claim in the avant-garde, recording with Jackie McLean and his own eccentric sessions, such as the aptly titled "Some Other Stuff." Steve Turre, a regular member of Woody Shaw's bands in the '80s, has sustained trombone on the current scene and brought to the instrument the modern vocabulary of Trane and Shaw. A host of younger players, such as Wynton's sideman Wycliffe Gordon, Frank Lacy, Conrad Herwig, and Robin Eubanks, are following suit.

Guitar, Vibes, and Organ

In addition to these alternative horns, there are several familiar jazz instruments that belong neither exclusively to the front line nor to the rhythm section. The guitar and vibraphone both play lead melodies the way a saxophone or trumpet would, but they are also both chordal instruments capable of comping behind another soloist. The organ is sui generis, a rhythm section instrument that provides its own bass and yet typically needs the support of a guitar's chords. Let's look at these hybrids in turn.

Jazz guitarists typically play a hollow-body instrument that falls somewhere between a strictly acoustic classical guitar and a solid-body rock guitar. The instrument is amplified but also produces much of its tone simply through the resonance of its empty body. The guitar was an essential ingredient in the rhythm sections of many of the best swing bands. Freddie Green in Count Basie's big band strummed a chord on every beat. Although he rarely soloed, his characteristic "bling, bling, bling" helped drive that band to swing as hard as it did. Charlie Christian was developing more of a reputation as a soloist at the same time in Benny Goodman's small groups. A transitional player leading the way toward bop, like Coleman Hawkins or Prez, Christian played single-line melodies in the fashion of a horn player.

But guitar wasn't given a voice to match the likes of Bird and bebop until the emergence of Wes Montgomery in the '50s. Arguably the greatest jazz guitarist ever, and certainly the most influential, Wes had a total bebop/hard-bop mentality on the instrument. A master of block chords and octaves, Wes nonetheless brought the guitar to the front of the band by playing circuitous bop lines in the tradition of Bird and Diz. Performing with all the bop masters of the day, like pianist Wynton Kelly and drummer Jimmy Cobb, he also participated in some of the most notable organ-guitar pairings with Jimmy Smith and even recorded more commercially with strings, as Bird had. Wes also paved the way for a host of postbop players, such as Kenny Burrell, Grant Green, and pop artist George Benson, who ranks as one of the finest pure jazz guitarists of all time.

During the period of the guitar's emergence as a major solo voice in jazz, the instrument was flourishing in rock and roll, and the crossover potential was felt immediately. Beyond Wes's more commercial adventures with strings, artists in the '70s began to incorporate rock elements—distortion and other electronic effects and funk beats—into jazz improvisations. John McLaughlin, Pat Metheny, and John Scofield have all experimented in this way and developed the guitar as a major crossover instrument in the world of fusion. There nonetheless remains a core group of straight-ahead traditionalists who keep the guitar in jazz's mainstream. Check out records by Freddie Bryant, Peter Bernstein, Russell Malone, and Mark Whitfield, and you'll be convinced that guitar has a place both in the acoustic and electric environments.

To most people's ears, the vibraphone is something like an overgrown xylophone. Using one or two mallets in each hand, the vibraphonist strikes metal bars that ring out with a chimelike reverberation. The marimba, by contrast, has wooden bars whose notes decay—peter out—instantly, rendering a more staccato effect. The vibes are also kind of a mongrel. At base a percussion instrument—more banging on things with sticks—the vibes can also sound chords and single-note melodies like a piano or guitar. The vibes were a familiar sight in the big-band era, largely due to bandleader and vibraphonist Lionel Hampton. "Hamp" would direct the entire big band with his vibes out front, laying out single-note melodies couched in the accompaniment of richly textured horn arrangements. In the small group, Red Norvo was doing the same thing with Benny Goodman and Teddy Wilson.

There is a Bird of the vibes, and he in fact played with Bird. Milt Jackson, known as "Bags," is one of the most naturally gifted improvisers in the history of the music. Swing and blues literally seem to drip from his mallets as he sways back and forth behind his instrument. Bags is the supreme bop player, capable of the virtuosic lines and syncopated rhythms characteristic of the genre. But he is also the ultimate blues player. I once saw his quartet, featuring Cedar Walton on piano, Ray Brown on bass, and Mickey Roker on drums, play an entire set of blues. Five tunes, all twelve-bar blues, all roughly the same medium tempo, and the music wasn't even remotely boring. Bags just continues to invent and invent on the instrument with his characteristic naturalness and élan.

With bop and blues as the constant, Bags has played in myriad contexts. He has recorded with Bird, with Trane, with Herbie Hancock, with young lions like Joshua Redman, and was a member of the longest-standing group in jazz history, the forty-year-old Modern Jazz Quartet co-led by Bags and pianist and composer Jon Lewis. He epitomizes what it means to swing, and you should catch him while he is still active.

Bags is such an overwhelming presence on the instrument that no subsequent vibes player can deny his influence. In the '60s, Bobby

Hutcherson became the next logical successor to Bags. Blessed with the same kind of natural creativity and swing, Hutcherson located the vibes in the context of the "new thing" of the '60s. Like Herbie Hancock or Wayne Shorter, "Hutch" stretched the limits of what a given chord might suggest melodically. He tackled the harmonically intricate tunes of the day and also recorded a number of free, almost classical twentieth-century pieces by drummer Joe Chambers. Sounding better than ever, Hutch is the quintessential modern jazz musician, capable of coaxing the best out of an Irving Berlin standard from the '20s, one of his own intricate compositions, or a free piece unbounded by form or chord structure.

A number of younger vibes players have emerged in recent years, most prominently Joe Locke and Steve Nelson, whose name appears on so many records these days, including my own. Steve shares in the tradition of Bags and Hutch—a natural improviser with seemingly endless harmonic and melodic resources—and is equally at home on a standard or a free piece. Something about the vibes, perhaps the unique combination of percussion and melody, seems to attract the best and most versatile musicians.

The organ is enjoying something of a renaissance in the '90s, and more and more pianists are turning to the organ as an alternative keyboard instrument. The organ, typically a Hammond B3, actually incorporates elements from many of the other rhythm section instruments. The organist's right hand plays lines like a pianist's, but the left hand typically walks bass lines in the lower registers, obviating the need for a bassist. Unlike the piano, the organ can create the satisfying low-frequency boom of a bass. The organist can also play bass lines with the foot pedals.

However, since the organist's left hand is occupied playing bass lines while the right hand improvises melodies, a harmonic "hole" is left open by the absence of a comping left hand. The piano player can play chords with his left hand to support the right hand's meanderings, but the organist's left hand is locked into a single-note groove with the drummer. That resulting harmonic hole is usually filled by a guitarist comping chords behind the organ solo. Guitar and organ fit naturally together; the guitarist comps for the organ solo, and the organist uses his or her right hand to comp for the guitar solo, all the while keeping a steady bass pulse with the left hand. The practical pairing of guitar and organ spawned some of the great combinations in the organ idiom, such as Jimmy Smith with Wes Montgomery, and George Benson with Lonnie Smith.

The legendary Blue Note record label, which has recorded much of the finest jazz since 1939, did much to popularize the organ in the '60s. Organ music is often about the blues, and Blue Note fostered that tendency by recording '60s groove masters like Jimmy Smith, Freddie Roach, Baby Face Willette, Shirley Scott, and John Patton. At the same time, Larry Young participated in the experimentation of the '60s by tackling more harmonically dense material and absorbing the influences of Trane and McCoy Tyner into the organ vocabulary. Listen to his *Unity* album on Blue Note, featuring Woody Shaw, Joe Henderson, and Elvin Jones, and you'll hear the organ's place in the modern Blue Note sound of the '60s.

Still, the organ never strays too far from the blues. Again, the nicknames and album titles tell the story. The current scene boasts "Brother" Jack McDuff and Richard "Groove" Holmes, and Jimmy Smith recently released a CD entitled *Damn*. Even newer exponents like Warner Brothers recording artist Larry Goldings are steeped in the blues and groove of the Blue Note organ sound of the '60s.

Singers

The jazz world has had a number of great female vocalists, from Billie Holiday and Ella Fitzgerald to Sarah Vaughan and Nancy Wilson—as well as male singers, like Louis Armstrong, Billy Eckstine, and Joe Williams. Vocalists occupy their own niche in the jazz ensemble, because most don't improvise the way instrumentalists do, and I have defined improvisation and swing as the two constants in the genre. Sarah Vaughan, blessed with perhaps the best human instrument in the history of the music, insisted that she wasn't a jazz singer, but rather an interpreter of popular song. The same might be said of Dinah Washington or Billie Holiday ("Lady Day"), both of whom could extract the best out of a familiar melody.

What marks these artists as jazz musicians? First, the best of them swing the hardest. Carmen McRae, for instance, had a tough, unsentimental edge to her voice, but she could make virtually any melody swing. Joe Williams with the Count Basie band could lead the entire orchestra into a bluesy frenzy on "Every Day I Have the Blues." Lady Day's impossibly relaxed phrasing was the perfect foil for Prez's suave tenor saxophone. In interpreting melodies, these artists phrased notes the same way that a horn player or pianist would.

Second, jazz vocalists improvise, albeit usually in a more limited way. The jazz singer is more likely than a vocalist from another genre to depart significantly from a composed melody. Check out how Betty Carter reinvents familiar melodies to such an extent that you recognize them only by the words. Some vocalists also improvise in the broader sense, extemporaneously "scatting" melodies and riffs like any horn player. Scatting involves improvising wordless lines and musical phrases with nonsense syllables—"ba skoodily bot" and the like.

Ella Fitzgerald may have been the ultimate *jazz* singer. A magnificent reader of standard melodies, Ella also had a swing feel as strong as anyone backing her up and could scat with the clarity, swing, and inventiveness of the best horn players. Jon Hendricks is the male equivalent in this regard. It's not surprising that some of the best scatters are indeed instrumental musicians who occasionally step out and sing. Trumpet great Clark Terry and tenor saxophonist Eddie Harris can reproduce with their voices the brilliant ideas they express with their horns. A week playing behind Eddie Harris, who, sadly, passed away in late 1996, convinced me that few singers could improvise any better.

Jimmy Katz/Giant Steps

Steve Wilson

Blue Note recording session, New York City
1996

The Set List

6

It's half past nine on Thursday night, and we are supposed to hit at ten. The club is the fabled Bradley's, a staple of New York's jazz scene for a quarter of a century and probably the most famous piano bar in the world until its recent closing. Alto saxophonist Steve Wilson and I are coleading a quartet with bassist Larry Grenadier and drummer Billy Drummond, and we are trying to decide what tunes to play. The long, wood-paneled bar and ivory-keyed Baldwin in residence at Bradley's have hosted many of the greatest musicians on the planet—pianists like Hank Jones, Cedar Walton, and Kenny Barron—and the club remains the after-hours hang of first resort for New York's musicians. You never know who'll show up as the evening progresses in this musical fishbowl, so Steve and I try to choose our repertoire carefully.

We opt to start the first set with a popular standard, Cole Porter's "Night and Day." Medium tempo, recognizable melody—that tune should be just about right as an opener for the savvy audience at Bradley's. We'll follow that tune with a *jazz* standard, Dizzy Gillespie's "Woody 'n' You," also known as "Algo Bueno." We'll play the "head," the melody that Dizzy composed, fast and with a samba feel, and then break into straight four/four. A popular standard and then a bop classic—so far, so good.

Dizzy's tune might get a little loud, so we should probably follow it with a ballad, but we can't agree on which one. I suggest "Round Midnight," Thelonious Monk's brilliant anthem from the '40s, but Steve wants to try another standard, "The Nearness of You," whose chord changes I barely know. We decide to choose between the two when we get there, and Larry the bassist will help me learn the harmonies if we play Steve's suggestion.

We do agree, however, that after the ballad, we should play something up-tempo and a little more modern. Billy suggests Wayne Shorter's "Yes or No," and we concur. Although it was written more than thirty years ago, that tune has both modal elements and definite chord changes, and it will allow the band to "stretch" and maybe play a little more "out." In other words, straight-ahead, but slightly on the edge. Finally, we'll close with a medium blues to chill things out a bit and set the tone for the second set.

Choosing tunes to play, or even to record, is one of those welcome burdens of being a jazz musician. Professional jazz musicians are expected to know from memory a huge stockpile of material drawn from American popular music, the historical contributions of jazz composers like Ellington and Monk, and more current tunes we hear and play at our "sessions," the informal jams we organize at each other's houses. The jazz repertoire is enormous, and no one musician knows it all, so the process of adding to one's arsenal of tunes is an unending quest. While I was on the road with Joshua Redman's band, bassist Christian McBride and I, both obsessive record listeners and self-proclaimed tune-smiths, used to play a kind of musical "name that tune" with obscure jazz compositions we had figured out off records. If one of us did not know the song, he was taught it by the other on the spot. Learning tunes, playing tunes you don't know well, is part of speaking the language of jazz.

But if jazz is improvisatory, why is the tune itself so important? Remember, for the most part, we improvise over song forms and harmonic structures. So when Steve calls "Night and Day," not only will the band play the familiar melody of that tune, but we will improvise over Cole Porter's song structure and chord changes. We're likely, of course, to mess with the harmonies and slip in and out of the melody, but the song's essential form and structure organize what we play. Other factors are at work, too. Some melodies are great to play, have a kind of swing built into them, and some sets of chord changes are also inspiring and challenging to improvise over. The underlying tune inspires the whole improvised performance.

But as our struggle to choose a set list illustrates, each song we choose is likely to influence every subsequent tune we play. Deciding on a set list, or deciding on the songs you will record on your CD, entails balancing moods, tempos, feels, and traditions. Bands usually try to mix tempos and keys, so that slow ballads follow up-tempo burners, and a song in C major—a "happy" or bright key—is juxtaposed to a somber E-flat-minor tune. We also try to coordinate styles and feels. A bristling samba may be followed by a loose, open waltz, and an ancient standard might pave the way for a modern abstraction. Eclecticism must be built into the set list, both to sustain the audience's interest and continually invigorate the improvising musicians.

Part of what makes learning the jazz repertoire such a wonderful chore is the wealth of cultural traditions it embraces. If you go to the Village Vanguard or any other good jazz club on any given night, you're likely to hear the influences of the full spectrum of American popular melodies, African and Caribbean rhythms, and classical romanticism. There is really no limit to the kinds of traditions jazz can absorb, and each artist or composer combines those influences in different ways. Wynton Marsalis's set might hark back to Duke Ellington and Louis Armstrong, whereas composer Donald Brown's tunes pay tribute to sources as diverse as Chick Corea and Kansas City's Jay McShann. My own pieces have a heavy dose of Monk and Wayne Shorter, while Christian McBride tips his hat in the direction of his hero, James Brown.

The sections that follow will introduce you to some of the rough categories of the jazz repertoire and its great contributors. As diverse a body of music as that repertoire comprises, musicians still tend to group tunes in classes. We talk about learning "standards" or knowing our "bop heads" or "Monk tunes."

Standards

I'm on the bandstand at Sweet Basil with saxophone master Eddie Harris, and the first two tunes went well. The audience seemed appreciative, and, more important, Eddie gave me a subtle nod of approval as the second tune ended. Then it all falls apart. He calls a forty-year-old show tune I barely know and insists that we play it in a funny key. The tune starts, I begin to fumble, and he turns around and whispers, "B-flat dominant, not minor!" I feel like hiding.

When the veterans of this business admonish younger players to learn "tunes," they are generally referring to American popular songs from the '20s to the '50s by composers ranging from George Gershwin to Richard Rodgers. These "standards," taken from the classic musicals and the pop hits of the day, have been a constant in the jazz repertoire from their first public exposure to the present. Eighteen-year-old pianists and bassists are expected to know their share of these songs, most of which were written decades before they were born, and young stars of this music continue to record standards that have been played a zillion times in the past.

Why the continued fidelity to songs whose general popularity faded long ago? Isn't there something stiflingly conservative about a band of twenty-three-year-olds playing an Irving Berlin song written in the '20s? Not by a long shot. For a host of reasons, the best standards have remained at the core of the jazz tradition, linking Louis Armstrong and Coleman Hawkins to student horn players struggling to commit tunes to memory in the dingy practice rooms of the Berklee College of Music. The great standards are, well, a standard by which successive generations of musicians test themselves. They are vehicles through which the next generation can say, "Look . . . this is how *we* play Gershwin. This is how *we* hear these songs." We, of course, don't limit ourselves to those standards, but we continue to revisit them as part of our inherited repertoire.

Liner notes to countless records and CDs boast that the artist in question "breathes new life into an old chestnut," to justify yet another recording of "Body and Soul" or "Autumn Leaves," but there is nothing to apologize about. Young musicians draw on the familiar repertoire to make a point. Just as we speak an improvised language we have learned from Duke and Bird and Miles, we sometimes choose similar source material, the same topics, to express our own personal point of view and to add, we hope, a fresh perspective. Standards not only link us to our musical ancestors but also pose the challenge of reinventing something otherwise so familiar. In a recent interview in *Downbeat* magazine, avant-garde reedman Marty Ehrlich averred that "How High the Moon" is not a piece of "dead music . . . it has by no means been exhausted."

Granted that standards are a key part of an evolving tradition, you might still wonder what's so special about these particular songs from a relatively narrow time period. Why not draw on more contemporary popular music? Plenty of jazz musicians have indeed recorded Beatles or Stevie Wonder tunes, and Herbie Hancock just released an album of jazz interpretations of rock hits entitled *The New Standard*. But the general reality is that younger jazz artists continue to look back to standards popular during their parents' youth. There are a number of factors at play here.

In the first place, the best standards are, in and of themselves, simply great pieces of music, whose melodies are inspiring to play. Irving Berlin, George Gershwin, Cole Porter, and Rodgers and Hart all wrote uniquely memorable melodies that captured the country's fancy for decades. Such composers represented a heyday of sorts in American popular music, and it wasn't simply the lyrics of these songs that inspired the Billie Holidays and Frank Sinatras to popularize them, but also the depth of emotion built into the music itself. No matter how many times you hear Gershwin's "I Loves You Porgy" and "Embraceable You," or Young and Washington's "My Foolish Heart," the best jazz musicians make those melodies speak with a fresh voice each time.

More contemporary popular music can of course be equally exhilarating or moving, but it generally is not as comfortable a vehicle for improvisation. For one thing, the chord changes of older standards lend themselves particularly well to improvising within the jazz idiom. It may be a matter of historical accident that the harmonies underlying Gershwin's "I Got Rhythm" have based more solos than just about any song, but the fact remains that these standards have good changes to play over, comfortably complex harmonies for the improviser.

More contemporary popular music has, on the other hand, quite intentionally moved away from harmonic structures characteristic of earlier pop tunes. Rock and pop have deliberately simplified their harmonic content in favor of other kinds of melodic or rhythmic lyricism. The result is that there are fewer harmonic resources in a rock tune than a standard for a jazz improviser to draw on. That distinction involves no value judgment. Beatles tunes and Rolling Stones tunes are great music. So are the works of Mozart and Prokofiev. But none of them have the types of harmonic structures that make them likely candidates for the jazz improviser.

But there are also less technical and more historical reasons for jazz's love affair with the standards. The flowering of American popular song in the '20s through the '50s happened to coincide with remarkable revolutions in jazz. The '20s and '30s witnessed the birth of improvisation in the modern sense. The '40s and '50s absorbed the shock waves of bop and postbop and the concomitant expansion of the improviser's freedom and rhythmic, melodic, and harmonic resources. During those restive decades of radical musical change, the popular source material of the day became inextricably bound up with the jazz musician's craft. Subsequent generations are, in a sense, still coming to terms with the innovations of those years and naturally look to the same source material, albeit with a more contemporary slant. In other words, it is no coincidence that the enduring standards were composed and popularized at the same time that jazz was evolving at an irrepressible rate.

The aftermath, happily, was not a tired adherence to an exhausted repertoire but an ongoing transformation and reinvention of jazz's source material. Miles, in particular, was famous for recycling the same standards in strikingly new ways. On *Something Else* with Cannonball Adderley, Miles recorded the ubiquitous "Autumn Leaves." Cool, laid-back, and swinging hard, the performance typified the sophistication and restraint of Miles's approach in the late '50s.

In 1964, someone recorded Miles's band playing the same tune live in Berlin, released on the LP *Heard 'Round the World.* The difference is startling. The tune is now an abstraction, swinging as hard as ever but meandering in and out of recognizability. Miles barely hints at the song's melody, slows the tempo down, and then starts punching out odd dissonant phrases. The rhythm section is constantly shifting rhythms and harmonies and effectively recomposing "Autumn Leaves." Whereas Cannonball's solo was a masterpiece of bluesy hard bop, Wayne Shorter's statement emerges from the interstices of the tune's changes and melodies. It, too, is a remarkably coherent abstraction. Less than a decade separates these two performances of the same tune by the same bandleader.

The standard, in other words, isn't a constraint but fodder for new invention. Check out pianist Bill Evans's numerous recordings of standards from the early '60s until his untimely death in the late '70s. Evans combined influences from Bud Powell to Debussy and was constantly able to reinvent the standards he played and recorded throughout his career. As a solo pianist in particular, he could coax the most moving, most touchingly romantic qualities out of a song simply by phrasing its melody in uncannily diverse and fluid ways.

The "standards" album has indeed become a benchmark of sorts in the modern jazz era. Pianist Keith Jarrett, bassist Gary Peacock, and drummer Jack DeJohnette are known as the "standards" trio because of the series of recordings they made of highly familiar tunes: "The Way You Look Tonight," "The Days of Wine and Roses," and similar material. They, too, have put an unmistakably personal stamp, a kind of open-ended melodic classicism, on tunes we have all heard before. In the '80s, Wynton Marsalis similarly recorded a series of albums designated *Marsalis Standard Time,* adding his own meticulous phrasing and quirky arranging skills to the standard repertoire. Just as trumpeter Bill Mobley writes intricate, involved arrangements of tunes like "Love

Walked In," the left-leaning avant-garde turns to similar tunes with a sense of appreciative irony.

Ultimately, standards are every bit as much a part of the language of jazz as Bird licks. They pose a ready challenge to new jazz musicians trying to find a personal voice and innovate within a shared tradition. Rather than marking jazz as a conservative idiom resistant to change, our tendency to turn to standards celebrates this music's endless capacity for transformation and renewal, for rethinking what we thought was so familiar.

Jazz Composers

Jazz's love affair with popular song is paralleled by a concurrent tradition of great composition. Even as Newk and Miles were obsessively recasting and reimagining the familiar resources of standards, composers were busy creating new source material, new improvisational challenges that shattered the musical rules and boundaries established by those standards. By writing their own melodies, harmonies, and rhythms, jazz musicians were able to create ideal vehicles for improvisation and transcend whatever limitations inhered in standards.

Over the years, music critics have been slow to acknowledge properly the legacy of great composition in jazz. It may be that the broader appeal and recognizability of standards have overshadowed the repertoire jazz has generated itself. Or it may be that, viewed as a purely improvised music, jazz still suffers from the misconception that the song the improviser is playing doesn't matter, since he or she makes the rest up on the spot. Indeed, the jazz composer has a doubly difficult task in creating a piece of music that sings on its own but that is also a springboard for improvised solos.

In any case, the critical world has finally come around. Jazz has, for better or worse, entered the "academy" of music schools and Ivy League "Intro to Jazz" classes. And ever since it became fashionable to deem jazz "America's classical music," the academic world that had once shunned the idiom has embraced jazz's best composers as some of the most important this country has contributed to twentieth-century music.

Virtually all of the great improvisers were also memorable composers. Bird, Diz, Miles, Freddie Hubbard, McCoy Tyner, Herbie Hancock, Trane—all could be as expressive with the pen as with their instruments. Nonetheless, certain composers stand out in the history of the music. These authors, too, wrote standards, *jazz* standards from within the music's own tradition, which every aspiring jazz artist must learn.

Duke Ellington represents for many listeners the pinnacle of jazz composition and arguably the greatest American composer of the twentieth century. Like Gershwin or Cole Porter, Duke wrote countless songs that became part of the popular musical culture of this country, such as "Sophisticated Lady" and "Don't Get Around Much Anymore." But unlike those popular writers, Duke was essentially a *jazz* composer writing for the considerable wealth of improvising talent in his various big bands. His focus, in other words, was to write not simply singable melodies but also compositions that could exploit the great improvisers in his groups. "Do Nothing till You Hear from Me" was originally entitled "Concerto for Cootie" in honor of trumpeter Cootie Williams. Duke's pieces were inspired by and were meant to inspire his band members.

As early as the '20s, Duke was exploiting the sonorous possibilities of the big band in innovative ways. Not only were the harmonies of Duke's underlying songs intricate and unpredictable, but the constant interaction of the various elements of the big band—the trumpets, 'bones, and saxes—changed arrangers' sense of each section's role in what was once considered to be the conventional dance band. Duke's regular collaborator, arranger and composer Billy Strayhorn, had the same kinds of sensibilities, and the result was a revolution, a transformation of dance music into highest compositional art.

Duke's expansiveness as a composer is almost overwhelming. In addition to popular songs like "Satin Doll" and "Take the A Train" (Strayhorn's piece), Ellington wrote a number of extended concert pieces, such as "Creole Rhapsody," "Black, Brown and Beige," and his religious suites of later years. If "Satin Doll" is whimsically hip, then "Single Petal of a Rose" is quietly majestic. There is virtually no mood or emotion that Ellington's pieces did not capture, and his legacy has influenced every jazz musician that followed.

Even though Duke was writing until the '70s, he is generally classed as a prebop, swing-era composer. When bop started to percolate in the mid-'40s, the great improvisers of the day began to incorporate the linear vocabulary of bop into their compositions. Thus Bird and Diz wrote numerous lines—basically fixed improvised melodies—over the chord structures of familiar tunes. "Ornithology" was Dizzy's tricky rewriting of the melody of "How High the Moon," and "Moose the Mooche" was Bird's permanent line over the changes of Gershwin's "I Got Rhythm." The stock analysis is that beboppers were trying to avoid paying royalties to the composers of the underlying standards, but there was likely a deeper aesthetic at play. If you were going to improvise in the radical new voice of bop, your compositions, even those based on standards, had to reflect that new vocabulary. Bebop tunes—almost all based on standard chord changes—are still very much part of the lexicon all jazz musicians must learn.

But while Bird and Diz may have been rethinking how to approach standard changes melodically, Thelonious Monk as composer was quietly dismantling assumptions about how melody, harmony, and rhythm interact. Monk was a study in contrasts. Rooted in the stride piano of Fats Waller and even James P. Johnson, Monk was sort of a traditional futurist. Many of his songs—"Hackensack" and "Nutty," for instance— are like nursery rhymes, with an almost childlike melodic simplicity; others—"Trinkle Tinkle" and "Criss Cross"—embody dense clusters of angular melodies, jagged rhythms, and harmonic dissonance. Monk was part of the bebop revolution, but even during the middle and late '40s, his compositions were already several steps beyond the lines-over-standards tunes his bop cohorts were writing.

Again paradoxically, Monk is simultaneously one of the most accessible and yet elusive pianists and composers in jazz history. Classic ballads, such as "Round Midnight," "Ask Me Now," and "Ruby, My Dear," seem to appeal instantly to even first-time listeners. So do the more playful anthems like "Little Rootie Tootie" and "Rhythmning." Yet built into those songs are harmonic depths and rhythmic and melodic quirks that musicians are still trying to assimilate. There are also more purely abstract compositions, like the startling "Skippy" and "Played Twice," which still sound unpredictable even after you have heard them hundreds of times. I have always loved Monk's music, but I still feel that I'm only just starting to "get" all that's there.

Like Duke, Monk is associated historically with a certain era, bebop, even though his originality transcends any particular movement. And despite years of radical innovation, Monk did not achieve the national attention he deserved until 1964, when he was featured on the cover of *Time* magazine. He had, of course, revolutionized jazz composition for nearly two previous decades, but the critical world was slow to embrace his authorial eccentricities. The current scene is still trying to come to terms with Monk. Sphere, Monk's middle name, was also the name of a fabulous group of the early '80s devoted to Monk's music; its members included pianist Kenny Barron, bassist Buster Williams, and former Monk sidemen drummer Ben Riley and tenor saxophonist Charlie Rouse. Many younger musicians continue to record and perform Monk's music, and I hear rumors that drummer Ralph Peterson has just completed an all-Monk record. We're not even close to exhausting the Monk repertoire.

The '50s and '60s witnessed the emergence of a number of fresh and influential composers. Onetime Jazz Messenger Horace Silver burst onto the jazz scene with a funky, gospel-tinged spin on the hard-bop vocabulary. After leaving Blakey's group, for whom he wrote classics like "Nica's Dream," Silver organized a series of small groups, mostly quintets, that gave voice to his brilliant writing. He is rooted in the bebop of Bud Powell, but much of his music incorporates Latin rhythms and a healthy dose of the blues—check out "Senor Blues" and "Song for My Father." Other hard-bop composers, such as pianist Duke Pearson and trumpeter Kenny Dorham, flourished in parallel with Silver and built up a vast reservoir of hard-bop standards still played today.

From a compositional standpoint, however, the '60s are noted not simply for the flourishing of a hard-edged kind of bop but for a remarkable and furious radicalism. Saxophonist Wayne Shorter is at the center of that innovation in composition. Like Silver an expatriot of Blakey's

Messengers, Wayne recorded a pathbreaking series of albums for Blue Note in the '60s featuring almost exclusively his own pieces. Wayne also recorded a host of his tunes with the Messengers and then with Miles's band in the mid-'60s.

Wayne's tunes moved several steps beyond what everyone expected from hard bop. The harmonies were far more sophisticated and abstract; seemingly unrelated chords and conflicting melodies meshed in a way that extended on the elusive integrity and logic of Monk's mosaics. Many of Wayne's most memorable works are his ballads—"Infant Eyes," "Virgo," "Penelope," "Iris," and "Miyako," which we'll check out in chapter 4—which meander from one strange progression to another in a bizarrely logical fashion. If you analyze Wayne's tunes on paper, you might scratch your head. If you simply listen to them, or immerse yourself in them as a player, the music will take your breath away. There are few contemporary writers in jazz who don't feel the towering presence of Wayne's pieces.

Wayne, for some, remains the greatest living jazz composer, and, as is the case with Monk and Duke, young jazz musicians continue to revisit his "standards." Other products of the '60s built on the radical power of Wayne's music in the ensuing decades. Pianist McCoy Tyner and trumpeter Woody Shaw wrote some of the most intense and gripping music of the late '60s and '70s. In more recent years, trumpeter Wynton Marsalis has combined the modernism of Wayne's harmonies with the classicism of Ellington-type orchestrations. Pianist Donald Brown—yet another former Messenger—may be the most important current writer on the scene, but others are emerging all the time. Just as jazz is experiencing an incredible influx of improvising talent, so too is the tradition of jazz composition being strengthened by an infusion of new writers. It's no surprise, after all, that great playing and writing go hand in hand.

PART III

A GUIDE TO RECORDINGS AT THE HEART OF MODERN JAZZ

Sonny Clark

Cover shot for Sonny's Crib, *Hackensack, New Jersey*
1957

Blowing Sessions
and Old Favorites

7

YOU NOW HAVE a whole arsenal of terms and concepts you can deploy to sound like one of the cats. Even if you only skimmed the earlier parts of this book, you can, in a sense, talk the talk, at least as far as a cocktail conversation about jazz is concerned. Drop the names John Coltrane and Art Blakey, talk about how a bass player walks, note that so-and-so has some serious chops, and you'll be deemed an aficionado.

But jazz is not a merely theoretical music, and you must earnestly listen to it to really develop a feel for how jazz works. Indeed, listening is about all you have to do, for, as I have stressed throughout this book, musicians and music lovers alike can only begin to speak the language of jazz by listening. Sometimes you listen without paying full attention, as when the music blares in your living room while you prepare dinner in the kitchen. That's fine, and it's part of a regular process of absorption. But sometimes you should sit down in front of your speakers—or at the Vanguard—and seriously check out what's happening among the musicians. We've talked about how it all is supposed to work and mesh together, but now it's time to listen and to hear.

Choosing ten recordings to discuss here is like choosing a sequence of tunes for the first set at Bradley's. There is so much music, such a huge breadth of expression that jazz encompasses, that it is extremely difficult to select just a few exemplary recordings. There are, of course, a host of collections and compilation records out there—one of the best is *The Smithsonian Collection of Classic Jazz*—but they are hopelessly limited by the sweeping ambition of their scope. The problem is not just that the selections reflect the subjective bias of their compilers, but that the music can be shortchanged in an effort to accomplish too much too quickly.

This book takes a very different, almost completely contrary approach. Rather than tackle a "Greatest Hits" or "Best of" project, I have deliberately chosen selections from a specific time period, the late '50s and '60s, and a limited class a postbop modernists who recorded primarily for the Blue Note record label. Why the self-imposed parameters?

First, one of the best ways to become familiar with a subject is to become expert in one area and then branch out from there. Most jazz musicians and fans began with a certain favorite era and clique of musicians. In my case, it was the pianists of the '30s and '40s, like Teddy Wilson, Earl Fatha Hines, and boogie-woogie master Meade Lux Lewis. Others began with Bird and bop in the '40s or the swing era in the '30s, or Wynton Marsalis in the '80s. That first focus acquaints you with the music, familiarizes you with its sounds, but also ultimately spurs you to look elsewhere for inspiration. One style of jazz inevitably serves as a link to what preceded and followed that style.

Second, it is sometimes easier to appreciate the diverse dialects of jazz by concentrating on one era and a particular set of artists rather than on the whole spectrum. Of course a Louis Armstrong record from the '20s will sound radically different from Chick Corea in the '70s. What may surprise you, however, is how strikingly different tenor players Hank Mobley and Wayne Shorter sounded playing similar material in the mid-'60s, or how much of a chameleon McCoy Tyner was performing in different ensembles during the same year.

Finally and most important, the music I have chosen is in no sense "limited." The '50s and '60s represent one of the most creative periods in jazz history, and it would take a lifetime to absorb that era's innovations. Moreover, that period has cast the greatest and most enduring spell over the current modern jazz scene. Ask any tenor player or trumpeter or pianist who their greatest influences are, and they are likely to reel off names that became familiar from the '50s on. Joshua Redman cites Sonny Rollins; Kenny Garrett just completed a CD of Coltrane's music; Wallace Roney invokes Miles; and Renee Rosnes speaks of her friendship with and admiration for Herbie Hancock. The '60s nourished our immediate musical ancestors, and that music remains at the core of what so many artists are trying to accomplish today.

I chose Blue Note records in particular because that label was consistently at the center of the jazz scene from the company's inception in 1939 to the present. In the late '50s and '60s, in particular, Blue Note signed and recorded the most creative and prolific artists again and again. The label did not have it all—Miles recorded for Columbia and Trane mostly for Impulse!—but most of the great players of the time, including Miles and Trane, participated in Blue Note records in one way or another. Blue Note's "house musicians" of the '50s and '60s, appearing continually on each other's albums, were at the heart of modern jazz.

Blue Note has historically been associated with a certain quality of straight-ahead jazz, the mainstream of hard bop and beyond. The label was never doggedly conservative—check out Ornette Coleman's free excursions or some of pianist Andrew Hill's avant-garde eccentricities—but it helped nurture the mainstream sound like no other label. Its recording engineer, the indomitable Rudy Van Gelder in Englewood Cliffs, New Jersey, was and is an integral part of that sound. Musicians still talk about getting a "Rudy" kind of sound on the piano or cymbals, and it was that distinctly warm and open acoustic quality that defined what recorded jazz was supposed to sound like for generations. Again, you'd be hard-pressed to find a current member of the mainstream jazz scene who doesn't own a wealth of Blue Note records or CDs.

One final note is in order. Musicians have certain pet albums that don't always square with the critically acclaimed recordings. Some recordings are classics by anyone's standards—Miles's "Kind of Blue," for instance, or Coleman Hawkins's reading of "Body and

Soul"—but others are references primarily for musicians. You rarely read critical evaluations of Lee Morgan's "The Procrastinator," but ask the cats and they'll tell you it's essential. I have tried to focus on recordings that are *musicians'* favorites, which may lack the critical visibility of better-known albums but which taught me and my contemporaries how to play. The list is, of course, endless and always evolving as we discover more material, but certain versions of certain songs continually come up in conversation. Let's check some of them out, starting with a "blowing session."

The blowing session is a staple in the recorded history of jazz. No complicated arrangements or dense compositional material. Get some great players into the studio, pick a few standards and some simple originals, and begin blowing and swinging. The blowing session is like an organized jam session. It doesn't require much rehearsal or specific preparation, but at its best, it reflects a lifetime of practice, commitment, and groove.

Blowing sessions were very much part of the identity of the music of the '50s and '60s. Hundreds of such record dates on Blue Note, Prestige, and other labels featured the top artists of the times, but the results were not always guaranteed. The blowing session is essentially a live gig captured in the studio, and like gigs, they vary in quality and inspiration. Great players don't always make great musical combinations, and some of these sessions sound more like the bad idea of an enthusiastic record producer than a coherent recording. But some blowing sessions are magical and epitomize the spirit of spontaneity and collaboration that is jazz. *Soul Station* is one such recording.

Hank Mobley, "Remember," from Soul Station (1960)

Soul Station, a Blue Note recording captured in Rudy Van Gelder's studio, is the essence of a blowing session. It has the relaxed intensity of the best improvisation and is a great primer in what unadulterated swing is all about. Like so many blowing sessions, it features a typical quartet—a tenor saxophone fronting the rhythm section—and a couple of standards, a blues, and a handful of simple originals. Nothing too intricate here, and the musicians on board were not the biggest names in their time, although they were among the most popular sidemen. *Soul Station* is not an all-star date by conventional standards, but an intensely democratic performance of the best in hard bop.

Let's begin by listening to Irving Berlin's "Remember," the first cut on *Soul Station*. Turn on your stereo, close your eyes, and listen to this simple masterpiece.

What did you hear? More appropriately, what did you feel? More than anything else, "Remember" swings extremely hard. Indeed, if you want to get a sense of what "swing" is, this cut is a good place to start. What else did you hear? Mobley's smooth and lyrical tenor solo built around Irving Berlin's simple melody, or Wynton Kelly's articulate statement on piano? "Remember" grooves hard—the rhythm section is definitely "tipping"—but not feverishly. It swings at a medium tempo with breezy élan.

Let's now get a little more specific about the players involved and their approach to Berlin's standard from the '20s. Hank Mobley— whom Dexter Gordon called "the Hankenstein" and the "middle-weight champion of the tenor"—was, according to the liner notes on the original LP, a "musicians' musician." Although he was not a revolutionary, like Newk or Trane, his sure sense of swing and melody led Art Blakey, Max Roach, Miles Davis, Horace Silver, and countless others to choose him as a sideman. Pianist Wynton Kelly was another first-call sideman and member of Miles Davis's band. Cannonball Adderley, who used Kelly on some of his own record dates, identified the pianist as one of the best compers around, and Herbie Hancock and McCoy Tyner acknowledge the strong influence of Kelly's bluesy snap on their playing.

Kelly is joined on *Soul Station* by his rhythm section mate from Davis's band, Paul Chambers. "Mr. P.C." (a nickname and the title of Trane's minor blues dedicated to Chambers) was *the* first-call bassist of the time, linking bebop and hard bop to the experimental modalism of the '60s. Finally, the irrepressible Art Blakey is featured on drums, here in the role of sideman rather than bandleader. Blakey played both roles fluently and frequently and has influenced virtually every modern-day drummer, from Tony Williams to Carl Allen.

The tune itself, while relatively obscure in the jazz repertoire, is as typical a standard as you might find. Comprising thirty-two bars, it exemplifies the standard AABA form: two identical "A sections," then the "bridge," or "B section," and finally a repeat of the A section. The descending harmonic pattern, or chord changes, is also simple and fairly basic fare, but the band makes the whole performance something special.

With no intro, Mobley starts right in on Berlin's melody, known as the "head" of the tune, a back-and-forth series of descending and ascending two-note intervals. Listen for the form of the tune; Hank states the first A and then starts again on the second A, slightly altering the phrasing of the melody. First time through, he begins the A section with "da doo-da, doo-da," but second time through, he says "da dooooooooo-da, doo-da," stressing that second note. In that simple choice, you begin to hear the germ of an improvisation and the importance of being able to state a melody with conviction and interest.

Throughout those two A sections, the rhythm section plays it pretty straight. Blakey is essentially keeping time, with the hi-hat emphasizing two and four—remember, you snap "one, TWO, three, FOUR"—and the cymbal spang-a-langing at a medium lilt. P.C. is "playing in two," or "with a two feel," during the first two A sections, not walking on every beat but playing the roots of the chords on one and three. The effect is something like "one (bass), two (hi-hat), three (bass), four (hi-hat)." Wynton Kelly pokes his characteristic chord voicings in the cracks between the melodic phrases. The whole sound is relaxed and in the pocket.

Then comes the bridge, or B section. Blakey introduces that section with a brief but thunderous drumroll, and P.C. starts walking on every beat. That shift from a two feel to walking should be pretty obvious, and even if you can't identify it in a technical sense, you'll probably feel the sudden opening up of the rhythmic textures, a sudden release into swing. After Mobley states the eight-bar bridge, the band returns to the final A section in a two feel and completes the "head" of the tune.

Mobley begins his solo with a "break"; at the very end of the head, after the final A section, Blakey strokes a quiet "rimshot" on the outer edge of his snare drum, and Mobley plays unaccompanied for two bars to introduce his solo. Hank's first chorus is again in a two feel, after which it breaks out into a swinging walking feel in four.

Check out how patient and logical Mobley's solo is. He starts with a simple series of ideas based on the tune's melody, with each improvised phrase suggesting the one that follows. From that tissue of ideas emerges a solo as coherent and ordered as Berlin's simple melody itself is. Hank was a master of spare lyricism, with few wasted notes. To return to the language metaphor, he was a thoughtful and considered speaker, not rambling but measured and focused. As the story he tells on "Remember" unfolds, Hank builds in intensity. His lines become denser and faster as the narrative reaches its denouement. He begins to "double up," to play sixteenth notes (which measure twice as fast as the eighth notes with which he began his solo), and the rhythm section follows along by increasing its dynamics and volume.

Listen closely to Hank's tenor sound as well. The '60s evokes images of radicalism and strident experimentation, but his sound harks back to the warmth and breathiness of the swing tenor players of the '30s and '40s. His hard-bop vocabulary notwithstanding, Hank had a certain softness and smoothness to his sound no matter how chaotic the accompaniment. Even as Blakey begins to play a "back beat," pounding away on the snare on two and four, Hank retains his smooth lyricism. His solo grows intense but never harsh or loud.

When Hank is finished, the rhythm section continues walking but brings down the volume for the beginning of the piano solo. Again, the idea is to let the soloist ease into his statement and to build up from a quiet beginning. Blakey was famous for admonishing the young musicians who populated his bands throughout the years to tame their enthusiasm and energy and build solo, to start at one level and end up somewhere higher. Blakey facilitates that approach on "Remember" by consciously bringing things down for the beginning of the piano solo.

Wynton Kelly is the perfect foil for Mobley. Similarly spare and relaxed in his approach, Wynton is known for his distinctive "lope," the bounce and groove in his playing. Like Mobley, he speaks in lucid ideas and has that rare gift of improvising lines that sound like little songs and melodies in themselves.

This approach is very much in the bop tradition of playing single note lines. Save for some octaves in the right hand, Wynton is a linear improviser speaking through hornlike lines rather than chords. His touch and sound in those single note lines are immediately identifiable to almost any pianist. There is a certain sparkling clarity to his attack on the piano. He is neither gentle nor heavy-handed, but always direct and to the point. Like Mobley's style, Wynton's is not about density or speed, but about lyricism and song. And his galloping lines never stray too far from the blues that rooted his playing.

P.C.'s bass solo completes the improvised sections. P.C. could play bebop lines on the bass with the facility of a horn player, and if you listen closely to his statement, you'll hear that his solo vocabulary reflects the same tradition as Hank's and Wynton's. When he is done, the full band takes the head out, from the bridge through the last A section, and Hank concludes with a brief unaccompanied "cadenza" to close the piece.

Now that we've focused on the head and the solos, let's go back and listen one more time. This time, however, our focus will be on the supporting cast. While Hank solos, check out the rhythm section, and while Wynton solos, check out P.C. and Bu. The key here is not the specifics of what they play, but the dynamics and support. As the solo gets louder or more impassioned, so does the rest of the band, which buoys what the soloist is doing while still affording him the space to take the lead. Hank is able to play in and around and against the rhythm section, and Wynton's left hand is bolstered by Blakey's propulsive beat. Throughout the performance, P.C. provides the impetus, the ski slope or the river current, that moves things along. It all grooves and flows together.

Don't worry if you can't sort out the technical details at first. Soon enough, you'll be able to tell the difference between the head and the solos, the A and B sections, and when the musicians are walking or playing in two. Listen to this simple performance ten times in a row, and you'll hear different elements each time. What you will likely hear right off the bat, however, is the swing feel these artists generate.

Sonny Clark, "Speak Low," from Sonny's Crib (1957)

"Speak Low," written in 1943 by Kurt Weill (who wrote *The Threepenny Opera*), is my mom's favorite standard. It's that kind of song, immediately accessible and memorable to anyone who has heard it once or twice. "Remember" was a rare find for Hank Mobley. "Speak Low" is much more part of the regular jazz lexicon, and any musician who doesn't already know it is likely to learn it the hard way, up on stage and in front of a discerning audience.

Certain songs have become "session tunes," pieces any jazz musician is likely to call at a private jam session or at the twilight session at Smalls, off Seventh Avenue South in the West Village. Some tunes—"Autumn Leaves," "Green Dolphin Street," "Stella by Starlight"—are so familiar that they generally elicit groans from the tired rhythm section. Sure, "The Days of Wine and Roses" is a great improvisational vehicle, but do we have to play it *again?*

"Speak Low" borders on that category but hasn't become quite so commonplace that musicians shy away from it. I heard Bobby Watson play it at Bradley's and thought, Hmmm, I'll have to start calling that tune on gigs again. Like "Remember," Weill's "Speak Low" also features an AABA form, but the A sections are twice as long, sixteen bars instead of the typical eight. That the tune's chord changes are always intriguing to play over may explain why the tune hasn't reached the dreaded "not again" status.

The performance of "Speak Low" we are going to check out also arose in the context of a bop blowing session, led by the wonderful pianist Sonny Clark. Like Hank Mobley, Clark was a musician's favorite, a versatile sideman and bebop swinger, but not a household name. Kenny Washington, one of the current scene's most knowledgeable and swinging drummers and a DJ for WBGO out of Newark, constantly points to Clark as one of the masters of his idiom. The lack of critical attention Clark has received in no way reflects the respect he commands among musicians.

The title of the album on which "Speak Low" appears, *Sonny's Crib*, betrays the performers' attitude toward the date. "Crib" means house or apartment, and, like the best blowing sessions, this record has the sound of an informal get-together or jam session. The record is in no sense disorganized, but, like Mobley's *Soul Station*, it has the casual spontaneity of a gig in a small club or a friendly rehearsal among the cats. Sonny's sidemen for the date were all future stars, in particular John Coltrane on tenor. The year 1957 marked a transitional time in Trane's career. He was already turning heads in Miles's bank but had not yet evolved into the spiritual pilgrim he would become during the '60s. You can already hear on this recording, however, the restless intensity of his playing.

The front line also featured trumpeter Donald Byrd and trombonist Curtis Fuller, two masters of the hard-bop idiom. Byrd, who had already been featured in Art Blakey's band, would go on to experiment with the electric sounds of funk and now fuses the rap and jazz genres into an emerging idiom known as "acid jazz." Fuller, who would join Blakey's band in the early '60s, took over the torch from J. J. Johnson as the most nimble bop improviser on the technically demanding 'bone. The rhythm section features P.C. on bass again, as well as Art Taylor ("A.T."), whose recent death robbed the jazz scene of one of its most swinging and captivating drummers.

After Clark plays a brief unaccompanied intro, the full band plays the head, the familiar melody of "Speak Low." You can immediately hear two key differences between the way Clark's band plays the head and Mobley's approach. First, the front lines sound different: Clark's band, which is a sextet, has a three-horn front line, as opposed to Mobley's quartet, where he stands alone on the frontline. "Speak Low" is simply but effectively arranged so that Trane's tenor sings the melody of the A sections while Byrd and Fuller play a harmonized and syncopated background. After Trane plays the tune's bridge, or B section, by himself, Fuller and Byrd return for the final A. Trumpet and trombone, both members of the brass family, blend smoothly in the background as Trane soars above with the melody.

Also note the changing feels during the head. Whereas Mobley plays the melody of "Remember" in a straight swing feel—first in two, then walking—Clark's band alternates between Latin and swing grooves. Focus on A.T.'s drumming throughout the head to hear the rhythmic shifts. After the intro, A.T. sets up a kind of rumba feel for the first eight bars of the A section. He's not playing cymbals, but banging out a percussive Latin rhythm on the sides and head of his open snare drum. The background voices of trombone and trumpet play a syncopated rhythm that meshes with A.T.'s beat. Then, for the second half of the A, A.T. swings for four bars and then returns to the rumba feel.

The technique of shifting feels during the form of a tune is something you will hear time and again during jazz performances. As you have already heard on "Remember," a band might switch between a two feel and walking in four/four, or between swing and Latin rhythms. Other possibilities are endless, and jazz musicians have experimented with virtually all of them—from cut time to double time, from one time signature to another, from Afro-Cuban to swing, and so forth. The objective here is to lend variety to a tune's rhythmic flow. Clark's arrangement of "Speak Low" may be simple, but the changing rhythmic texture adds excitement and unpredictability to a song so many already know so well.

At the end of the head, the band breaks and Trane roars in with his solo. What a difference from Mobley! Here are two tenor players of roughly the same generation, playing only three years apart, and no doubt influenced by the same predecessors. Both were sidemen for Miles Davis and regular participants in the postbop scene of the late '50s and '60s, and yet it's hard to believe they are playing the same instrument.

Let's focus on the sound first. Remember Mobley's tone: smooth, a little breathy and buttery, and warm and a little dark. Trane's solo features the antithesis of that sound. Even as he states the melody of "Speak Low," you can hear how much brighter and more incisive his tone is. If Mobley is softer and a little diffident, Trane is riveting and in your face. By no means harsh, but forcefully direct and gripping. Trane was throughout his career a magnificent ballad player, but until his untimely death in 1967, he maintained and perfected that grab-hold-of-you sound.

Indeed, Trane's sound heralded a more modern approach to the saxophone. Whereas Mobley came from the warm tradition of Ben Webster, Hawk, and Lester Young, Trane started his own tradition of a brighter and more aggressive sound. Those different approaches shine through in today's players. Some opt for the warmth of the older tradition, while others, like Michael Brecker, prefer the steely clarity of Trane.

Arguing about the relative merits of the different tenor sounds is, incidentally, no idle academic exercise. Those tones are vital to the sound of jazz as a whole. If I turn on the radio and either Hank or Trane is playing, I can identify the tenor player in only a few notes by the tone alone. What's more, you can do it, too. Go out and buy some Hank and Trane records, and you will begin to hear the consistent differences. If you can recognize the difference in vocal qualities between one singer and another—pop, opera, whatever—you can certainly recognize horn players. Trane's sound, so distinctive and modern, is a good place to start.

Beyond the tone, you will immediately recognize the unbridled fire of Trane's solo approach. Again, let's use Mobley as a basis for comparison. Hank is terse and understated, full of a kind of quiet and engaging passion. Trane is explosive. After his simple break, he almost immediately starts "doubling" up, playing sixteenth-note phrases over the medium-tempo groove. In other words, rather than playing standard eighth-note phrases—two notes for every quarter-note beat of the tune's pulse—Trane plays twice as fast, with four notes per beat. Mobley leads up to some doubling up at the end of his "Remember" solo, but Trane flutters along at double time throughout most of his one-chorus solo on "Speak Low."

Of course, speed alone is nothing more than a technical accomplishment within the reach of most studious sax players. The nature of Trane's note choice is also remarkable. First, like Mobley, he was a superb changes player, and no matter how rapid-fire his approach may have been, he was keenly aware of the tune's underlying harmonic structure. The "Speak Low" solo is a case in point, because Trane is as changes conscious and harmonically astute as the bop masters, like Clark and P.C., who also participate in this performance.

Notice how Trane exploits the huge range of the saxophone. He plays the melody of "Speak Low" in the upper register of the tenor's range but then sweeps through the entire spectrum of notes during his solo. His lines start low, swing up high, and then redescend. The melodic intervals are similarly startling, as Trane bounces from a high, near screech to a lower honk. His performance here is indicative of the incredible freedom Trane brought to the horn. All registers were fair game, and assumptions about technical limitations—such as the ability to jump instantly from a high to a low note—were shattered. At the same time, Trane brought a new measure of eloquence to the horn, a vocabulary equal to the task of expressing the endless flow of ideas that coursed through his artistic imagination.

This 1957 sideman recording is just a preliminary glimpse of what Trane is all about. Check out the dates with Miles in the '50s or the increasingly intense Impulse! recordings in the '60s. Some of those recordings—*Transition*, *Sun Ship*, and *First Meditations*, all in 1965, for instance—are so impassioned and explosive that your stereo may appear ready to topple over. And yet, even in the context of those more untamed dates, where most of the tunes are based on a simple vamp over a single chord or scale, Trane's music remains beautiful and lyrical. The jazz community is still coming to terms with Trane three decades after his death in 1967, and the numerous recordings he made are a great place to ground your explorations of modern jazz.

After Trane's solo, Curtis Fuller and Donald Byrd split a chorus, with Fuller playing the first two A sections and Byrd finishing up with the bridge and final A of the chorus. Note the difference in brass sounds. Fuller always had the ability to make the stentorian trombone sound lithe and agile while maintaining its full-bodied presence. The 'bone is a lower-register instrument with a kind of visceral impact, but Fuller's articulation and phrasing give the instrument a swinging bounce. At the end of his brief statement, Fuller also doubles up with a flurry of cleanly articulated bop lines.

Byrd's half chorus provides a ready comparison with Fuller's trombone tone. While the trumpet and 'bone are both brass instruments, the trumpet is designed to cover higher registers than the 'bone. Because it has valves rather than simply the slide of the trombone, the trumpet is faster and less technically limited than the bone. Byrd's warm tone in a sense sounds like the trombone moved up to a higher register. Remember that distinctive brass sound of 'bone and trumpet, and it will help you distinguish among the different jazz horns. Byrd also speaks in the bop vocabulary, and his swinging half chorus reflects the influences of Dizzy Gillespie and Clifford Brown.

Sonny Clark takes over for the next full chorus. Clark is very much part of the same scene as Wynton Kelly but is even more purely bebop. He shares a number of traits with Kelly—crystal-clear phrasing and a bluesy bent—but Sonny comes directly out of the tradition of Bud Powell, Al Haig, and other master bop pianists. The word itself—"bebop"—was an attempt to capture the syncopated phrasing of the idiom. A bop line might conclude "ba-skoodily be-bop." The accenting and phrasing, the triplets and landing on the offbeat all marked bop as the modern vocabulary, and present-day musicians remain firmly rooted in bop. Check out how Clark navigates the changes of "Speak Low," bouncing and swinging his way through the chorus. Indeed, there is a definite continuity between Byrd's solo and Clark's. They are both speaking in the same bop tongue, and it is as if Sonny takes over the conversational lead based on what Byrd said.

After the band takes the tune out, skip back to the beginning of "Speak Low" and, just as you did with "Remember," focus on the rhythm section, on Clark's comping, P.C.'s walking groove, and A.T.'s beat. Listen to the chatter on A.T.'s snare drum. While the cymbals spang-a-lang throughout the piece, A.T.'s snare provides a constant commentary that meshes with Clark's comping and the soloists' meanderings. Remember, the rhythm section grounds the whole performance and lays the rhythmic carpet over which the soloists stroll. Clark, P.C., and A.T. were a world-class rhythm section and very much typify what the swing feel of hard bop was all about.

Clifford Brown, Curly Russell, Lou Donaldson, and Art Blakey

Birdland, New York City
1954

The Blues

8

"But can he play the blues?"

THE BLUES ARE a kind of benchmark for all jazz musicians. Even if you are a technical wizard or know every standard ever written, at the end of the day you still must be able to play the blues. Of course, not every jazz musician has to be "bluesy" in his or her approach, and we will indeed hear some less than stereotypically "bluesy" blues. Still, as a final measure of excellence and authenticity, many of the most modern and even abstract players remain rooted in the blues. A number of classic albums, such as saxophonist and arranger Oliver Nelson's landmark *Blues and the Abstract Truth* and Trane's *Coltrane Plays the Blues*, are devoted specifically to exploring different approaches to the blues.

Oddly enough, "the blues" is a potentially ambiguous and confusing term, especially for a nonmusician. In its broadest sense—and a sense only tangentially relevant to a discussion of jazz—the blues is an idiom of music distinct from jazz, classical, rock, and the like. B. B. King and Clarence Gatemouth Brown are blues artists; Duke Ellington and Bird are not, even though they repeatedly recorded various blues tunes throughout their careers. While that form of "blues" has historical and cultural ties to jazz, it exists as a separate entity from the music we are discussing in this book.

The blues from a jazz musician's perspective denotes first and foremost a particular song form and set of chord changes. Like Gershwin's "I Got Rhythm," the blues is simply a chord progression that lends itself extremely well to flexible and extended improvisation. In a sense, the blues form is the ultimate standard, the most frequent set of chord changes to which jazz musicians turn again and again, as both a performance and practice vehicle. When I'm feeling very industrious, I might practice for hours playing over a single blues in the key of F. Louis Armstrong, the Count Basie Orchestra, Duke Ellington, and virtually every name band leading up to the swing era recorded tunes based on blues changes. The blues structure is also integral to bop and underlies numerous bebop melodies, such as Bird's "Relaxin' at Camarillo" and Monk's "Straight No Chaser."

The basic blues is a twelve-bar form organized around certain defining chord changes. You can acquaint yourself with the harmonies of a basic blues by referring to the chart on page 109. There are endless variations on these changes, hundreds of ways to add and substitute different harmonies, but certain relationships must remain for the song to qualify as a blues. For instance, note that after the first four bars of the chord F seven, the root of the next chord jumps up three notes in the scale to B-flat seven, or the "four chord." That harmonic movement, from the root chord up to the four chord, is one of the essential ingredients of the blues form. Even if you don't recognize it in a technical or theoretical sense, you would certainly miss that change if it were absent.

One easy way to become familiar with the basic twelve-bar blues form is simply to count bars. Listen for the pulse of the tune, the "one, two, three, four" hump of the bass beat, and count measures. After some practice, you will probably be able to hear each chorus as a unit of twelve four-beat measures. You also may begin to hear the consistency of the harmonic progression, a basic song form that links a Meade Lux Lewis "boogie-woogie" blues of the '30s to a Coltrane blues of the '60s.

But the blues, even within the limits of the jazz genre, means something much more than a twelve-bar song form, and here we once again

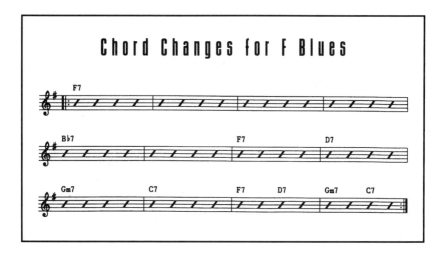

Chord Changes for F Blues

encounter elusive notions of a feeling and a spirit. Even as it denotes a particular musical structure, the "blues" also evokes a certain spiritual and soulful way of playing. Indeed, you can play as "bluesy" as a gospel choir without actually improvising over a strict blues. The late pianist Bobby Timmons, another Blakey alumnus, and the still-active vibraphonist Milt Jackson imbue virtually everything they play with the blues, and some of jazz's bluesiest anthems, like Timmons's "Moanin'," have little to do with a blues song form.

Almost anyone familiar with American music has some visceral sense of what playing "bluesy" is all about. Again, the euphemisms abound. A bluesy player is "funky" or "churchy"; he or she plays "soulfully" and with a lot of "grease." The church, where artists like Timmons honed their craft, is an important source of the blues, where religious passion translates into musical expression. Food imagery also comes into play when describing the blues. Beyond the grease, you might hear a bit about "biscuits and gravy" and "greens." Organist Jimmy Smith's legendary record, the funky *Back at the Chicken Shack*, captures much of this spirit.

It's time to check out some blues, one quite deliberately funky and the other conspicuously not so. Both performances are masterpieces of blues improvisation, and the radical differences between them underscore the huge potential of the blues as a springboard for improvisation.

Art Blakey, "Blues," from Live Messengers (1954)

Side four of my old Blue Note LP *Live Messengers* lists the second cut as " 'Blues' (author unknown)." Critic Ira Gitler's liner notes describe this track similarly: "as traditional as you can get and credited to no one for precisely that reason." Blakey et al. simply played a blues one night at New York's fabled club Birdland—also known as "The Jazz Corner of the World." Although the piece had no preset or recognizable melody, it was rooted in the vitally important tradition of the blues.

This particular band predated Blakey's series of Jazz Messenger groups, which would come to serve as the paradigm of small-group modern jazz. Bu, of course, had played with virtually everybody, and that same year, he was beginning to perform and record with the musicians who would formally become the first Messenger group. Those classic Messengers played tightly knit and intricate arrangements of original compositions or rewritten standards. "Blues," by contrast, is just a live jam-session piece, a product of something even more informal than a studio blowing session.

This particular quintet had as many strong ties to the past as it did links to the decades to come. Bassist Curly Russell was a veteran of Dizzy's and Bird's bands, and, even more so than Blakey himself, was firmly rooted in the bebop revolution of the late '40s. The rest of the band was younger and more raw, poised to take Bird's vocabulary into the next era.

The piece starts with an eight-bar piano intro spearheaded by pianist Horace Silver. Silver's music, both as a much-lauded composer and as a fiercely percussive pianist, comes straight out of the blues and gospel, and as you hear one audience member exult, "Horace, oh Horace!" you sense the room slide inevitably into the groove of a slow blues. More on Horace later in this section.

Alto saxophonist Lou Donaldson begins the actual soloing—remember, the band doesn't even bother with a formal melody here—with an unmistakable reference to Bird's "Parker's Mood," one of the most recognizable slow blues in history. Donaldson, still very active and vocal today, was one of Bird's immediate descendants, firmly grounded in the language and phrasing of bop but with a bluesier slant. "Sweet Papa Lou," who went on to record a number of extremely funky records under his own name for Blue Note, is a hilarious and daunting presence in the clubs today. With the authority that comes with his link to the golden age of modern jazz, he serves as a kind of Don Rickles to the jazz community, a relentless critic liberally opining on who can and can't play.

His falsetto put-downs are legendary. After drum great Jack De-Johnette recorded an album on piano, Lou is reputed to have said, "Oh, you a piano player. That's how come you can't play no drums." When one young alto player, now a fixture in the avant-garde community, told Lou that he too was from St. Louis, Donaldson responded, "You oughta be playing more horn if you're from St. Louis." According to Donaldson, "Trane can't play no blues," "McCoy's just got a gimmick," and "women can't play jazz." No one takes the barrage of insults too seriously, but we all respect his incredible skills as an improviser.

Lou's solo is doused in bop and blues. For the first four bars, he teases different phrasing out of the same "Parker's Mood" reference, then begins to double up over the slow beat. By the end of the first chorus, he is already blistering the surface of the blues with a flurry of bop statements. He begins his second chorus with an ascending flutter that has become a blues signature for alto players. Cannonball would play the same lick years later, speaking the inherited language we discussed earlier. For the remainder of the next two choruses that complete his solo, Lou keeps up in the same spirit, alternating between repeated blues phrases and the syncopated melodies of bop.

Check out how clean and articulate his phrasing is. Remember, the alto is a higher-pitched instrument than Mobley's and Trane's tenor, and Lou negotiates its upper register with remarkable clarity and ease. Add to the bite and precision of Lou's phrasing the bright sweep of his big sound. Aside from Lou, only a very few alto players—maybe Cannonball and Phil Woods—have had that sparkling pop in their sound.

Young trumpeter Clifford Brown takes over after Lou finishes his four-chorus statement. Killed in a car crash in his twenties, "Brownie"

left a remarkable recorded and spiritual legacy for succeeding generations of musicians. He was one of Dizzy's heir apparents and brought to
the horn an even bigger sound and flawless phrasing. Virtually every
trumpet player who followed—Donald Byrd, Lee Morgan, Freddie Hubbard, Woody Shaw, and Wynton Marsalis—points to Brownie as a
breakthrough player and major influence.

Like Donaldson, and indeed like most musicians dealing with a slow
blues, Brownie tends to take a phrase and twist and squeeze it. Something about the tempo and the groove makes you want to play around
with an idea and coax different colors out of essentially the same notes.
Brownie picks up Lou's last phrase and mimics it as he swaggers into his
first chorus. He shoots up high briefly and then ends the chorus in the
horn's lowest and most growling register. He begins the second and then
the third chorus with the same "repeated idea" approach. Take a phrase,
toy with it, "grease" it up some, and move on to your next thought. The
whole thing is completely funky.

At the beginning of Brownie's fourth and final chorus, the rhythm
section plays in "stop time," landing with a short note on the first beat
of each of the first four bars and then leaving the rest of each bar silent.
Brownie saunters through the stop-time breaks as if he knew they were
coming, although he probably didn't. Throughout, check out the different timbres Brownie elicits from the trumpet. When he's down low,
he rumbles. When he's in his comfortable midrange, there's an almost
breathy warmth to his sound akin to the great tenor saxophonists.
When he's up high, the horn literally crackles with percussive power.

Horace Silver's presence is potent even before his solo begins. During the horn solos, Silver's comping functions like a big-band section,
buoying the soloists and punching through like a brass background. Silver's solo itself is straight blues and funk. Even more than Lou and
Brownie, whose statements are steeped in the rapid-fire phrasing of
bebop, Silver just plays the blues, plain and simple, like a pianist accompanying a gospel chorus. If the horns nimbly dance their way around
the twelve-bar form with the harmonic and rhythmic idiosyncrasies of
bop, Horace sticks to the basic blues scale and simple chords. His solo

is all about rhythm and groove, and he, too, gets a stop-time feature at the beginning of his last chorus.

Incidentally, you'll want to check out the wealth of great recordings Horace made under his own name for Blue Note. Like Blakey, Silver always featured a stellar front line, with artists ranging from Hank Mobley and Blue Mitchell to Woody Shaw and Michael Brecker. More important, Horace's compositions, which mirror the fierce rhythmic drive and funky aesthetic of his playing, are some of the greatest in the modern jazz repertoire. Pieces like "Song for My Father," "Peace," and "Nica's Dream" are de rigueur jazz standards.

After Silver's solo, the horns complete the performance with a jointly improvised final chorus, sliding around each other and wrapping up the groove. It's the perfect rousing finish to a perfect impromptu performance. Blakey's "Blues," as typical and unrehearsed as anything you might hear at a late-night jam session, captures the spirit of the blues and the spontaneous conversation it inevitably inspires among jazz musicians.

Chick Corea, "Matrix," from Now He Sings, Now He Sobs (1968)

When I purchased Chick Corea's Now He Sings, Now He Sobs and dropped the needle on the opening tune, "Matrix," for the very first time, I was a little disconcerted by what I heard. Was this tune supposed to be a blues? It seemed about as far removed from Blakey's "Blues" as I could imagine. The melody wasn't very funky, at least not in the traditional sense, and although Chick's trio seemed to be playing in twelve-bar phrases, the blues changes were only barely discernible. Pianist Mulgrew Miller and others had passionately recommended the album to me, but I was frankly a little nonplussed. What was up with this recording? It wasn't "out" or avant-garde in the typical ways, but it sounded so different from what I was used to hearing.

That record would ultimately change the way I and so many others approach the piano and chord changes and the blues. Dogged by some critics when it was first released, *Now He Sings, Now He Sobs*, with its poetic title and quirky compositions, is a benchmark recording of the basic piano trio. Its leader, Chick Corea, is one of the best musicians ever to have graced the jazz scene. In the mid-'60s, playing with hard boppers like trumpeter Blue Mitchell, Chick came out of the tradition of Bud Powell and Wynton Kelly. Within just a few years, Chick would start down a different path, exploring free jazz and the avant-garde, Latin rhythms, and ultimately electric fusion and traditional classical music.

Now He Sings, Now He Sobs documents Chick at a critical time in his career, when he was making his move away from the typical Blue Note sound he had cultivated earlier in the decade of the '60s. Still oriented in the chord changes and, for the most part, formal song structures, Chick was starting to stretch out. "Matrix" is another wonder of crossbreeding, a traditional blues expressed in a freer and decidedly more modern format.

Like the leader himself, Chick's band mates in the trio are musicians of remarkable breadth and versatility. Roy Haynes is a kind of Miles of the drums. He recorded with bop master Bud Powell in the early '50s but would go on to slash his way through some wild recordings with Trane and eccentric pianist Andrew Hill, as well as to lead his own groups to the present day. Most young drummers still consider Roy one of the most inventively "modern" and hip of all jazz percussionists. Like Corea, bassist Miroslav Vitous is featured on one or two classic '60s Blue Note sides, in particular with trumpeter Donald Byrd. Vitous, too, would adopt a freer approach in the ensuing years.

"Matrix" is a small puzzle of a piece. Its opening four bars sound like an ascending sprightly nursery rhyme, completely tonal, bright, and happy. The next four bars, when the band ostensibly moves to the four chords of the blues form, are by contrast a dissonant convulsion, almost a spasm of angular and shattered chord clusters. Finally, the last four bars return to the nursery rhyme, this time played as a descending figure. Note how Roy Haynes negotiates the melody, punctuating and filling in the cracks between the play theme and the dissonance with his cymbals and snare drums. The whole statement of the melody is as catchy as it is unnerving, and even a seasoned musician unfamiliar with the tune might not immediately recognize it as a blues.

Listen closely to Chick's phrasing at the beginning of his soloing. For the first chorus, the trio plays with a two feel—Vitous emphasizing the first and third beats—but then it shifts into a straight four/four. Chick's sound and touch on the piano owe much to McCoy Tyner's lucid attack (for more on McCoy, see chapter 10), but Chick is even more precise, even cleaner and brighter sounding. During the solo, he tends to focus on the highest registers of the piano, and his lines ring out with a bell-like clarity.

The solo also mirrors the split personality of the head of the tune. Much of the time, Chick is laying out clean, pretty lines, sweeping in and out of the chord changes in keeping with the playful spirit of the opening melody. He periodically interrupts those lines, however, with fierce, rattling chords and rhythmic bombs. Perhaps the title "Matrix" has something to do with this slightly schizophrenic intersection of two musical characters.

Recall also that this melding of themes and moods is taking place in the context of the blues. Chick is ostensibly playing the same set of chord changes that Brownie and Lou Donaldson use in Blakey's "Blues," but the effect is totally different. Chick is still, for the most part, "in" the changes, but he has departed from the bop vocabulary for a more scalar and modal approach. Taking his lead from Trane and McCoy, Chick treats the chord changes as rough road maps for a certain sound and tonality, rather than a directive for what notes "fit" the chords in conventional harmonic terms.

The most remarkable thing about "Matrix" may be the dynamic control of the rhythm section as a whole. During Chick's solo, Roy Haynes keeps up a kind of propulsive commentary that seems just barely to hold the proceedings in check. The effect is akin to a pot about to boil over. Roy's cymbal beat and sound, whose lucidity and precision are the perfect foil for Chick's attack, somehow manage to ratchet up the intensity with every chorus but without resorting to bashing or exploding. Roy's approach to swinging also takes bebop—which he had a strong hand in perfecting—several steps farther. The beat he plays on his cymbals is far more broken up and far more unpredictable than the insistent grooves we have heard with Blakey and Art Taylor. As suggested with other recordings, listen to "Matrix" one time while focusing exclusively on the drums. You'll hear that the spang-a-lang rhythm has been exploded into a thousand rhythmic elements.

Vitous's accompaniment and virtuosic bass solo provide another excellent frame of reference for comparison. With P.C. and Curly Russell, we heard bass lines grounded in the language and harmonic textures of bop. For those bassists, walking and soloing were all about playing the changes and keeping up the groove. Vitous is much freer and more likely to depart from the expected notes and harmonies. He is also more melodically angular, concerned less with just "tipping" and more with chasing Corea's and Haynes's rhythmic choices around the finger board of the bass. During his own solo, Vitous deftly toys with repeated phrases. The vocabulary is no longer the basic blues à la Horace Silver, but an open-ended twelve-bar form in which the blues are only just suggested. After freely strumming his way through several choruses, he walks his way into Corea's return.

The band completes the solos with Chick and Roy "trading" choruses, each taking turns playing twelve-bar fragments. Listen to the various sounds Roy is able to coax from his drum kit—exploding cymbals, bass drum bombs, and snare drum thwacks. Even though drummers don't play notes with pitches in the traditional sense, Roy's choruses are deftly melodic. He and Chick are engaged in a conversation, each picking up where the other left off. After Chick trails off in his final chorus, the band plays the "Matrix" theme twice to end the piece.

Blakey's "Blues" and Corea's "Matrix" represent two extremes in approaches to the blues. One is funky, down-home, and totally and instantly familiar. The other is abstract, quietly explosive, and sometimes only suggestive of what we think of as the blues. And yet, as different as these two recordings are, they are linked by a common song form, a relatively narrow slice of time in the artistic chronology of jazz, and by players like Blakey and Haynes who are closely associated with the same era in this music. Jazz is about communication through the medium of improvisation. Jazz musicians, starting with the same base material, naturally express themselves in different and uniquely personal ways. "Blues" and "Matrix," so closely linked and yet so aesthetically different, offer a glimpse into how truly transformative that language of improvisation can be.

Francis Wolff/Mosaic Images

Sonny Rollins

Sonny Rollins Vol. 2, *Hackensack, New Jersey*
1957

Ballads

9

AFTER YOU'VE PLAYED a medium standard, a blues, and an up-tempo burner to start out the set, you need something to chill the proceedings out. You need something a little less aggressive and more alluring, less in-your-face and more intimate. Or maybe the entire quintet or sextet has been taking extended solos on the first several pieces, and you want to feature the pianist or the tenor player for one tune. Blakey always used to call once-a-set features for the individual horn players or pianists in his bands. In these circumstances, you inevitably call a ballad to change the pace and mood.

Ballads are—for lack of a more graceful characterization— slow and pretty. The typical ballad is taken at a devilishly slow tempo, without the walking bass drive of a faster swing tune or the insistent groove of a Latin-tinged piece. Ballads are also by nature lyrical, and listeners are more prone to close their eyes than tap their feet. The best ballads are, of course, anything but watered down or "soft." Listen to "Dearly Beloved" on Trane's *Sun Ship*, and you'll hear an almost primal rumble under Trane's impassioned statement. The musical intensity and emotional commitment are still there, sometimes even more so, but that intensity is quieter and more focused in a ballad.

Ballads are also great testing grounds for jazz improvisers.

The ballad form requires more patience and more concentration on the part of the player, and all the chops in the world won't rescue you from harsh scrutiny if you don't have the maturity and confidence to play lyrically as the moment requires. Indeed, it is a truism among musicians that younger and less experienced players are more fumble-fingered on ballads. It's relatively easier to run your licks over a faster tune; but when the persistent chatter of the drummer's cymbals and bassist's walk are pared down to brushes and a quiet bass pulse, the soloist and her shortcomings are totally exposed. The tenor player's tone, the trumpeter's vibrato, and the pianist's chord voicings and touch are all ruthlessly laid bare to a now-silent audience.

It's not surprising that many of the greatest ballad players are also among the most patient and thoughtful soloists. Tenor saxophonist Dexter Gordon, always swinging but never conventionally flashy, drew the best out of ballad melodies. His capacious, breathy sound and gentle phrasing brought out the romance of familiar melodies. Pianist Bill Evans had a similar gift. Despite his considerable skills on the piano keyboard, Evans relied on lush harmonies and a sensitive touch in approaching the ballad form.

Many of the ballads played by jazz musicians are part of the standard repertoire. These include themes from popular movies and theater in the '30s, '40s, and '50s. Cole Porter, Rodgers and Hart, Gershwin, Alec Wilder, Jerome Kern, and Sammy Cahn all wrote great songs that fall into this category. Singers, too, love these kinds of songs, because they are filled with an old-fashioned romantic sensibility. There is, however, a parallel strain of important ballads composed by the great jazz writers, such as Duke Ellington and Billy Strayhorn. Like the ballad soloist, the jazz composer faces the challenges of a slower tempo and a quieter setting, where the minutest details are examined under a microscope. Duke and Strayhorn could withstand such intense scrutiny because their songs were so powerfully logical and beautiful.

We're going to listen to ballads by two of the most important composers in the history of modern jazz—or all jazz, for that matter. Wayne Shorter and Thelonious Monk both reinvented jazz composition. Apparently receiving signals from another musical planet, they heard sounds and colors never imagined by their predecessors or anyone since. Choosing their "best" pieces is difficult, since so many of their compositions are now jazz standards we all play regularly. Both were incomparable creators of ballads. Like so many great writers, they brought a composer's sense of form and coherence to the solos through which they interpreted those ballads.

Wayne Shorter, "Miyako," from Schizophrenia (1968)

One of Wayne Shorter's many gifts as a composer was his ability to link unusual harmonies and chord structures in unprecedented ways. The combination of exotic chord movements with gentle melodies made Wayne's ballads seem musically startling on paper, but in performance, they sound inevitable and familiar.

Like other records discussed in this book, Wayne's *Schizophrenia* is a musician's record and reference. Not necessarily the subject of much critical attention, *Schizophrenia* is the type of recording musicians talk about and obsess over. Certain tunes from the record have become quasi-standards, such as the funky "Tom Thumb," but more than anything else, the record as a whole sustains the type of "vibe"—a moody collective personality—that is so difficult to capture in the recording studio. Among the album's most "vibey" and memorable pieces is Wayne's tender waltz, "Miyako." A number of other musicians have recorded the piece, but it's not a tune everyone knows.

The first quality to recognize about "Miyako" is that it is a waltz. A waltz is simply a piece in three/four time, rather than the conventional four/four. Waltzes can be fast, medium, or, as in the case of "Miyako," taken at a ballad tempo. When you first listen to the piece, try to discern the waltz time signature. Measures are not divided into the typical "one, TWO, three, FOUR" phrases, but rather "ONE, two, three; ONE, two, three." The pulse is slow, so try to hear where each beat falls.

Far more important than the technical presence of the waltz beat, however, is the seductive mood of the entire performance. Its opening phrase is sultry and inviting, but the piece is also touched by a certain sadness and diffidence. It's as if Wayne steps out front to make his opening statement, then shyly retreats into introspection. Much of Wayne's music has that same thoughtful and momentarily revealing quality. In the case of "Miyako," the combination of a spare melody of long tones with a rich underlying harmony sustains the vibe.

Much of the performance's power lies in the relative absence of extended improvisation. Whereas what we have listened to in previous chapters is all about improvisation and building solos in intensity, "Miyako"'s vibe derives from the composition itself. Indeed, the recording embraces only four choruses: The head is stated twice, Wayne improvises for one chorus, and then the band restates the melody. With only one-quarter of the piece devoted to improvised soloing, Wayne's recording is more about interpreting a composed melody than blowing over a set of chord changes.

Although the record features a sextet, Wayne's band mates on the front line play only a supporting role for the tenor melody. James Spaulding on alto saxophone and Curtis Fuller on trombone—Fuller had teamed up with Wayne and Art Blakey earlier in the '60s and was the 'bone player on Sonny Clark's "Speak Low"—were among the most frequent of Blue Note sidemen. They epitomized the spitfire intensity of hard bop and participated in numerous legendary recordings. Here, after Wayne plays the first half of the head of "Miyako" with the rhythm section only, Spaulding and Fuller play a harmonized background for the remainder of the song form. Their quiet backdrop does much to enhance the moody development of the piece.

It is, however, Wayne and the rhythm section of Herbie Hancock on piano, Ron Carter on bass, and Joe Chambers on drums that make "Miyako" so special. Check out the way Wayne and the rhythm section work together to invest each chorus of the melody with a slightly different flavor. As opposed to the more conspicuous invention of a full-blown solo, listen closely to how Herbie and Wayne nudge each other through the three choruses when the tune's melody is played relatively "straight." The band is still improvising in a technical sense—there is still an extemporaneous decision making in everything Wayne and the rhythm section play—but rather than using the song structure as a blueprint for improvisation, the band is simply interpreting and reinterpreting the piece's melody.

Take the drums, for instance. Joe Chambers plays quiet brushes the first time through the head. He provides a swishy backdrop and occasional cymbal accents to highlight the peaks and valleys of the melody. Then, moments after Wayne returns to the opening theme for the second chorus, Chambers switches to sticks and an entirely different nine/eight feel. In other words, rather than playing the straight, slow three/four of the first chorus, Chambers subdivides each beat into three triplets; each measure of "oooone, twooooo, threeeee" becomes "ONEtwothree, TWOtwothree, THREEtwothree." Whatever the musicological description, you can easily hear how that choice radically changes the feel of the piece. Chambers's delicate nine/eight cymbal beat makes everything sound brighter and quicker-paced, even though the underlying tempo remains unchanged. Chambers is himself a master composer of everything from straight-ahead jazz pieces to twentieth-century abstractions, and his composer's sensibility made him the ideal foil for many of Wayne's Blue Note records.

If you return to the beginning of the recording, you'll hear that Herbie and Ron similarly dance around "Miyako" 's form. While Wayne states the basic melody, Herbie constantly improvises subtle counter-melodies in the piano's upper registers in call-and-response fashion. Those background phrases never interfere with the simplicity of Wayne's melody, but rather keep the deliberately slow pace moving steadily forward. Ron does the same thing. His bass lines respond to Chambers's rhythmic shifts and Hancock's musings. Even though he is there to provide the harmonic and rhythmic foundation for the band, Ron, too, contributes a sense of interactive melody to the performance. The overall impression is that, as Wayne states the haunting line of the piece, the rhythm section engages in a quiet, gentle conversation about that line.

Wayne has an idiosyncratic solo style that matches the way he speaks. In interviews he pauses, thinks—comfortable with the silence—

and then suggests a compelling metaphor to describe his idea. During an interview Wayne considered a comment that Trane's frenetic solo style sounded too much like "scrambled eggs." Wayne paused, then said, "But it's how you scramble those eggs."

When he steps out and solos on the third chorus of "Miyako," he scrambles the piece's basic melody in a most fascinating way. The solo starts with a yearning cry and a downward interval and then, like the composition itself, recedes into a reticent meditation. Throughout his brief solo, Wayne makes regular reference to the formal melody of "Miyako," scrambling and embellishing its contours with improvised themes, but never departing very far from the composition's form or line. There is almost nothing in the solo resembling a conventional bop line or a Tranelike sweep. Wayne could certainly play in that style, as he frequently demonstrated with Blakey and Miles. His "Miyako" solo is, in contrast, a series of sounds and thoughts, rather than lines in the conventional sense.

One of the most elegantly spare moments of the entire performance happens midway through Wayne's solo. When he reaches that point in the song where the other horns would come in to support the melody, Wayne plays a single note, A, and Herbie responds with an ascending phrase. Wayne then drops an octave and plays the same note, and then another octave and again the same A, with Herbie continuing to ascend. One simple note in three registers is hardly something sax students would bother transcribing, and yet the combination of Herbie and Wayne in effect comping for each other is breathtaking.

At the end of his chorus, Wayne shifts seamlessly back into the melody, and the band plays the tune out until the final, unresolved chord. The cliché of "less is more," of "leaving space," is nowhere more evident than in "Miyako," where the band makes each silence between notes as significant as the phrases that surround it. As opposed to Trane's flurry of notes or Chick's clanging clusters, Wayne's perform-ance is more suggestive and understated, but the passion is still there. The performance, like its final unresolved chord, is a question, inviting your imagination to fill the interstices between quiet phrases.

Sonny Rollins, "Reflections," from Sonny Rollins Vol. 2. (1957)

I have always thought that tenor saxophonist Sonny "Newk" Rollins and pianist Thelonious Monk were a perfect match, each rooted in bop but both wildly angular in their phrasing and rhythmically volatile. Both were revolutionaries and yet operated paradoxically at the heart of the jazz mainstream. They did not play or record together all that much, but their occasional collaborations were clearly mutually inspiring.

Monk, like Wayne, was such a prolific genius of a composer that it is difficult to home in on his best pieces. There is no weak material compositionally as far as Monk is concerned, and just his ballad repertoire overshadows most composers' entire output. "Round Midnight," "Ruby My Dear," "Crepescule with Nellie," "Ugly Beauty," "Ask Me Now," "Monk's Mood," "Light Blue"—the list of his classic ballads goes on and on. Even as every piece is radically different and unpredictable, each seems to share Monk's playful and slightly warped proclivities.

"Reflections" is perhaps a corny title, the kind of appellation you affix to a generic "pretty" song. There is, however, nothing sentimental or trivial about the piece or how Monk and Newk perform it. Like so much of Monk's music, it combines something very traditional and familiar sounding with a certain jagged lurch. It almost seems to be poking fun at itself and tweaking the sentimentality of its title and a few of its phrases.

Monk's solo piano introduces the piece. Starting with his trademark whole-tone scale—a sequence of notes each spaced a "whole step" apart—the intro is almost heraldic, kind of a "here we come, get ready" series of announcements. It is also, in classic Monk fashion, a little off-center and dissonant, and the octave smashes that complete each phrase warn us that traditional ballad sentimentality will not follow.

As I mentioned earlier, Monk's style sprawls across a number of musical traditions. He was very much a creature of the stride piano tradition of Fats Waller and Earl Fatha Hines, heroes from the '20s and

'30s, and yet came up as a player and professional with the bebop icons, Bird and Diz. Even in the late '40s, however, he was already reaching beyond the bebop revolution and incorporating a new kind of harmonic and rhythmic approach that was full of strange clustered chords and discordant melodies. Modern pianists are still coming to terms with Monk's twisted approach, and they know exactly what a bandleader wants when the directive is to play "Monklike." Monk had a way of weaving his eccentricities into a profoundly musical voice, and the song title "Ugly Beauty" captures much of the spirit of his playing. His brief piano intro on "Reflections," which announces the piece with a kind of clumsy majesty, brims with these paradoxes.

After the intro, Newk and the indomitable rhythm team of Blakey on drums and Paul Chambers on bass—the same pair who backed Hank Mobley's "Remember"—come in with the melody. Newk's throaty tenor sound is typically arresting and larger-than-life. During this period, the late '50s, he was occasionally dubbed an "angry" tenor player, because his sound was so gruff and his phrasing so potent. But anger hardly describes his treatment of Monk's melody. Like the pianist, Newk adopts a sound and approach that are at once pretty and startling, and although he treats "Reflections" with the requisite degree of tenderness built into the piece, he seems to share Monk's unsentimental aesthetic as he plows through the melody.

The opening phrases of "Reflections," and indeed the bulk of the composition, are relatively traditional. The chords are generally standard fare, laid out in a thirty-two-bar AABA form, and the melody tracks the harmonies closely. But even though the piece has none of the wild tangles of Monk tunes like "Trinkle Tinkle" or "Skippy"—both blizzards of crazy phrases—there are several hints of Monkian explosions. Midway through each A section, for instance, Newk jumps up an octave with a declaratory "dah da-dee-da!" that shatters any expectations you might have. All the while, even during the melody's tamer moments, Monk's quirky comping maintains the same sense that you simply don't know what's coming next.

Monk's solo, which begins immediately following the quartet's statement of the tune's melody, shares something fundamental with

Wayne Shorter's ballad approach. Both players remain fairly faithful to the composed melody of the underlying song rather than simply running licks over the tune's chord changes. Indeed, they improvise as much over and around the melody of the ballad as the underlying chord changes. Also like Wayne, Monk was comfortable with and even drawn to silence and dissonance where you would expect otherwise. Another master egg-scrambler, Monk builds drama as much through space as through clutter.

Monk's solo, spurred by Blakey's double-time beat, is basically a reinterpretation of the simple melody of "Reflections." He twists and turns the essential notes and phrasing, but constantly refers back to the head that Newk played. Part of the spirit of his solo is an almost deliberate looseness and sloppiness, a willingness to clang his way around the tune's form. What a different approach from that of Sonny Clark, Wynton Kelly, and Chick Corea, all masters of the brisk single-line phrase! All were rooted in bop, but Monk—who is supposed to be one of bop's inventors—actually sounds more chordal, more orchestral, and less concerned with the intricate phraseology of bebop. Rather than negotiating his way through the chord changes like a nimble-fingered horn player à la Kelly or Clark, Monk playfully bangs out the melody of "Reflections" and punctuates it with raining runs and shattering chord clusters.

Yet there is an unmistakable continuity at work here. Remember Chick's "Matrix," a nursery-rhyme ditty interrupted by a convulsive cluster? Chick is a great admirer of Monk—the current release of *Now He Sings, Now He Sobs* in fact contains a version of Monk's "Pannonica"—and his "Matrix" is very much in the Monk tradition. Compare "Matrix," an "out," or dissonant, blues, and "Reflections," an ostensibly tender ballad. The two pieces, separated by more than a decade, are wildly different, and yet you'll hear how Chick drew on the Monk tradition of coupling something directly and accessibly melodic with something a little more outrageous. Monk's romp through his "Reflections" solo defines a whole idiom of piano playing that draws on the instrument's percussive and orchestral potential.

Newk takes over for his own solo in much the same spirit as Monk.

He, too, makes constant allusion to the basic melody of "Reflections" and sustains the craggy spirit of the whole performance. Even more than Monk, he alternates references to the song's melody with explosive bursts that span the full range of the horn. Note how often he starts a phrase with a low-register honk and then bursts upward to a pinched high note. The tenor saxophone's answer to bop and Bird, Newk on this particular recording is nonetheless in Monk's playground, full of unexpected bumps and falls. Like the song's composer, Newk approaches the piece with a split personality, alternating between the tender and the eruptive.

Among other qualities—the enormous sound and melodic imagination, for instance—Newk is simply one of the swingingest improvisers in history. Partly due to the authority of his tone, Newk's notes always have a percussive impact and "pop" that give his lines the rhythmic drive of a drummer. And while "Reflections" is ostensibly a slow-paced ballad, once Blakey begins to urge Newk on with a double-time feel and propulsive chatter on the drums, Newk is in full swing mode. Each of the double-time phrases he sings between fragments of the tune's melody gives the slow tempo an inexorable forward momentum.

Ballads are by definition slow, so each chorus takes relatively longer to play. It is accordingly common practice to shortcut a ballad after the last solo by going straight to the bridge, or "B section," of the tune and thus playing only half of the song on the way out. Monk does exactly that in "Reflections," following the conclusion of Newk's chorus with a restatement of the bridge and Newk's final take on the last A section. Notice how Newk leads into that final A section with a huge, splashy leap up and down into the melody. Newk plays the last A out, and the band rolls to a halt on a final, unresolved chord.

If Shorter's "Miyako" is reclusive and dark, Monk's "Reflections" is more of a romp and a frolic—not exactly the introspective and meditative piece suggested by the title. Maybe because they are slowed down and laid bare, ballads more than other idioms often closely reflect the personalities of their interpreters. Wayne is a high-intensity player, to be sure, but his style has always been cerebral and moody. Monk's music is always in some sense beautiful, but in a more whimsical and childlike way. "Miyako" and "Reflections," both as compositions and as improvised performances, give you a glimpse into those personalities and will help you recognize the consistent voices these two masters bring to everything they write and play.

Francis Wolff/Mosaic Images

Lee Morgan

Hank Mobley's A Caddy for Daddy *session, Englewood Cliffs, New Jersey*
1965

South, East, and West of the Border

10

WHILE IT HAS loyal adherents the world over, jazz is at heart an American phenomenon. It was born here with Louis Armstrong in the '20s, or perhaps even earlier with Scott Joplin's ragtime, and its evolution reflects the struggles and triumphs of American artistry and black Americans. Some, like critic Stanley Crouch, have even suggested that the jazz band is the embodiment of the American democratic ideal. It invites and thrives on equal participation and input from each contributing member.

The big cities of the United States are also some of the best places to hear and see jazz. There are, of course, wonderful clubs in Paris and Tokyo, and spectacular open-air jazz festivals throughout Europe. Moreover, it has become an unfortunate truism that European audiences are often far more open-minded and welcoming to the American jazz musician than U.S. clubs and festivals. The gigs even pay better across the pond. Still, jazz flourishes in the Unites States. Stroll down Seventh Avenue South in New York City, and you're liable to hear some of the greatest musicians alive performing on any night of the week. There is a sense of community and history in New York that draws and keeps jazz musicians here.

And yet, like New York City itself, jazz is a kind of cultural melting pot, an international mongrel. From its very beginnings, American jazz has sought out the rhythms, melodies, and harmonies of the international scene. European classical music has a profound influence on modern jazz, and legends from Charlie Parker to Bill Evans all pay homage to the harmonic riches of Stravinsky and Debussy. The influence of Eastern music, with its odd rhythmic meters and twisted scales, also shines through the improvisations and compositions of Woody Shaw, John Coltrane, and tenor saxophonist Billy Harper.

But perhaps no international music has cast a more enduring spell on the American jazz artist than the rhythmic textures of Africa, Latin America, and the Caribbean. Those three traditions are, of course, widely disparate, but they often coalesce in the imagination of the jazz improviser. The African tradition has been a constant throughout jazz history. Certain early Duke Ellington pieces were built around the sound of the jungle, replete with growling trumpets and roaring trombones. Many modern drummers, like Art Blakey, made the pilgrimage to Africa to study its rich tradition of complex rhythms, and John Coltrane's classic quartet of the '60s merged Trane's increasing devotion to Islam with a ritualistic African chant.

Latin influences, and South American influences more generally, have been incorporated into the African aesthetic. Dizzy Gillespie may deserve most of the credit for merging the two traditions. His collaborations with percussionist Chano Pozo earned the moniker "Afro-Cuban" for the way they combined African and Cuban rhythms, and his two masterpieces, "A Night in Tunisia" and "Manteca," have become anthems of that rhythmic style. We heard a taste of those kinds of rhythms in A.T.'s rhumba beat during the head of Sonny Clark's version of "Speak Low." The sound is now very much part of the jazz mainstream.

The Caribbean rhythms of Calypso, which entered the jazz lexicon with Sonny Rollins's "St. Thomas," have also been integrated into the Afro-Latin tradition. Rock and funk beats have become part of these "south of the border" sounds of jazz as well. Purely Latin sounds thrive, too. What we think of as the salsa rhythms played by Latin dance bands are very much part of the jazz drummer's arsenal, as is the bossa nova, a product of Brazil and composers like Antonio Carlos Jobim. Tenor saxophonist Stan Getz, who recorded much of Jobim's music, is largely responsible for popularizing the bossa nova, but that tradition has also become a staple of the jazz repertoire.

All these various rhythmic influences are loosely, and probably erroneously, dubbed "Latin" by jazz musicians. If you ask the bandleader what kind of groove or feel she wants, the likely answer is either "swing" or "Latin," with some kind of modifier. It might be "a bossa" or "straight eighths" or "twelve/eight," but Latin in the first instance distinguishes the feel from the traditional swing beat. It's still jazz, whatever the description, and as you'll hear in the three pieces that follow, each of the various grooves can swing as hard as the most basic spang-a-lang.

McCoy Tyner, "African Village," from Time for Tyner (1968)

McCoy Tyner is a towering giant of modern jazz piano and composition. Just as pianists sometimes try to play "Monklike," I've had countless bandleaders ask me to give them "a little McCoy." Although he could and did play in the best bop tradition when the context required, in the '60s McCoy came up with an utterly new way of approaching chord changes and improvisation. As a member of Trane's classic quartet and a leader of his own magnificent Blue Note and Impulse! sessions, McCoy—like Bird and Monk and Trane—invented a radically different vocabulary that shattered assumptions about how the piano was to be played.

McCoy's music is about majesty, power, and matchless intensity. A searcher and a prober like Trane, he was the perfect complement to the saxophonist's spiritual quest. Indeed, it is hard to imagine any other pianist who could have kept up with Trane's urgency, much less inspired him the way McCoy did. Less authoritative voices would have folded, but McCoy thrived in Trane's maelstrom. We've described Monk and Chick as playful, and Wynton Kelly and Sonny Clark as lucid. McCoy is volcanic.

Much of the power and fervor that marks Tyner's music lies in its spiritual underpinnings. McCoy is a devout Muslim with a strong cultural affinity for Africa and its rhythms. His album titles reflect the cosmic and ethnic roots of his influences: *Expansions* (1969), *Sahara* (1972), *Song of the New World* (1973), and *Enlightenment* (1973), for instance. The same can be said for his song titles: "Search for Peace," "Passion Dance," "Utopia," and "Man from Tanganyika." The classic LP *Extensions* (1970) features a *National Geographic*–style album photo of an African tribe and four impassioned pieces entitled "Message from the Nile," "The Wanderer," "Survival Blues," and "His Blessing." As the names suggest, McCoy's musical vision involves a search for utopia—for peace, passion, and artistic enlightenment.

McCoy's LP, *Time for Tyner*, captured this artist at the peak of his powers as both a player and composer. Having left Trane in 1965 and experienced the anguish of his death in 1967, McCoy embarked on a series of remarkable albums as a leader. Many of those albums, both for Blue Note and then Milestone in the '70s, featured larger ensembles with multiple horns and even string sections. *Time for Tyner* is, by contrast, a simple quartet date with vibraphone hero Bobby Hutcherson, bassist Herbie Lewis, and drummer Freddie Waits. The forceful impact of the music, nonetheless, belies the group's size.

"African Village," the longest cut on the album, begins with an extended and dramatic introduction of bass and drums. Herbie Lewis begins with "double stops" on the bass, two notes played simultaneously like a chord. He slides up in "fifths," notes separated by five intervals in the E-minor scale, in a repeating ostinato or "vamp." Waits on drums establishes the African-flavored three/four pulse of the tune. Yes, "African Village" is a waltz, but with a decidedly different feel from Wayne Shorter's gentle "Miyako."

After the double stops, Lewis begins strumming high notes on the bass, and the other band members—either McCoy or Bobby Hutcherson or both—add a small shakerlike percussion instrument and cowbells as Waits's insistent drumbeat grows more intense. The focus here is on rhythm. The notes Lewis plays do not matter so much as the building up of rhythmic power and density. Waits begins to slam loudly on his tom-toms—now you can hear the origin of the name of that particular piece of the drum kit—and introduces another bass ostinato by Lewis in preparation for the beginning of the melody.

As bass and drums sound ready to explode, McCoy and Bobby charge in with the melody of "African Village." Like Trane, McCoy had a penchant for the "pentatonic scale," a five-note pattern derived from the full minor scale. In this case, for example, the pentatonic scale reads E, G, A, B, and D. The A section of "African Village" is built entirely around that scale, which gives the melody both an African and nearly Asian or Eastern flavor. The bridge, by contrast, is constructed around the "diminished" scale, in which notes are alternately separated by half and whole steps (one or two adjacent notes). If the pentatonic scale sounds Eastern, the diminished bridge bristles with drama and suspense. Like the introduction, the bridge builds a level of tension that makes the transition to the next section, here a return to the A section, a necessary and vital release.

Throughout the head of "African Village," listen also to how McCoy and Bobby play the melody in tight unison. Although not played to a strict swing beat, "African Village" has that sense of "lift" and relentless forward thrust discussed earlier. The propulsive feel derives not only from Waits's strong African groove but also from the crisp attack of vibes and piano in stating the melody together. Listen closely to how McCoy fills in the spaces between the song's phrases. It is as if all the villagers are coming together for a rapturous celebration.

At the close of the tune's head, McCoy and Herbie Lewis set up a bass vamp—the same as heard in the intro—to usher in Bobby Hutcherson's solo. The vibes, like the piano, is a combined percussion and melody instrument. The vibraphonist plays notes and scales just as a saxophonist or pianist would, but in this case by hammering on metal bars with mallets. On the vibes, it's also possible to sustain a note and let it ring out. You can hear all these qualities in the beginning of Hutcherson's solo. He bangs out a clarion opening phrase that concludes with a long, ringing note. His first chorus sustains this spirit by weaving in and out of the powerful rhythmic texture supplied by the rhythm section. He does not so much solo over the rest of the band as work his way into the swirling African rhythms.

Bobby plays one ABA chorus based on the chord changes of the tune, but then the band shifts into a straight modal vamp. As mentioned earlier, "modal" playing involves improvising over simply one or two chords or scales, rather than an intricate structure of chord changes. Indeed, the formal structure of "African Village" is basically built around the two scales discussed above, although a pattern of chord changes underlies those scales. Here, after Bobby's initial chorus over the song's form, the band simply improvises openly on E minor or the "E Dorian mode"—technical music-speak for the scale involved. There is no set chorus length or number of bars, but rather simply a sound the band can explore.

Listen closely as Hutcherson moves in and out of the basic tonality. Hutcherson was one of the harmonic and melodic whiz kids of the '60s, able to create something vastly complex and intriguing with the simplest of base material, and, conversely, to pare intricate harmonies down to their essence. On the E-minor vamp of "African Village," he plays simple melodies, blindingly fast runs, and shimmering trills. He also departs frequently from the basic E-minor sound to set up dissonances and tensions, in a sense improvising new harmonies over the simple E-minor sound. The challenge in modal playing, which Hutcherson meets so excellently, is to take a simple scale and speak freely and creatively through it. Hutcherson builds the interest and variety in his solo through a dense mix of melody, rhythm, and phrasing.

After Bobby fades out of his solo over the E Dorian vamp with a trill, McCoy eases into his solo by basically restating the melody of "African Village." McCoy has been a thunderous presence throughout the performance so far, and his comping has all the forcefulness of an aggressive drummer. McCoy's initial restatement of the piece's melody at the beginning of his own solo—something we have heard in the improvisations of Wayne, Monk, and Newk—offers an immediate glimpse into how fiercely rhythmic his attack is. As each note and chord rings out in clarion fashion, his signature left hand drops bombs of fifths or octaves, lending a powerful bottom end to his expansive sound.

Think about the different piano sounds we've heard. Sonny Clark and Wynton Kelly were smooth and lucid, whereas Monk was deliberately discordant. Horace Silver was all funk, while Chick Corea had an almost classical level of precision. McCoy is an amalgam and exaggeration of all these approaches. Certainly lucid and precise, and often jarringly dissonant, his sound is probably the most percussive in jazz history. Possessed of big hands and powerful arms, McCoy often treats the piano like a large drum kit with a thunderous bass drum and crystalline cymbals. He is, in fact, a master ballad player and composer capable of great romance, but on pieces like "African Village," where rhythm is paramount, he is also a percussionist.

Remarkably, McCoy is simultaneously one of the most harmonically sophisticated of pianists. Like Hutcherson, and in keeping with his apprenticeship with Trane, McCoy can extract an amazing number of colors and harmonies out of a simple mode. After punching his way through a melodic restatement of "African Village," McCoy solos over the simple E-minor tonality or mode. He also weaves in and out of that mode, often playing harmonies and notes that are deliberately "wrong" and that create tensions with the basic sound we expect to hear.

As he explores the open vamp on E Dorian, McCoy develops a trancelike fixation with certain phrases. He plays a simple melody or phrase and teases it apart, wringing from it other possibilities. The phrase begins to expand outward and ultimately explodes into its component parts as McCoy sweeps through the full range of the piano. His simple single-note phrases boil over into powerful, ratting chords. Indeed, the whole solo has this quality of exploring the microdetails and expanding outward. At base, "African Village" is a chant, where the participants focus on a simple image as a window to a larger vision.

Herbie Lewis completes the soloing with his bow. We have not heard the bow in previous pieces, but the principle is the same as that for a violin or cello. Here, the low-pitched drone of Lewis's bowing is the perfect complement to Bobby and McCoy. Like the other soloists, Lewis steps forward out of the rhythmic wash to meditate publicly on the E-minor vamp. He then switches back to plucking and returns to the introductory bass ostinato to reintroduce the melody. The entire band returns to play the head out and vamps climatically until a crashing close.

"African Village" evolves like the celebration of a village community. It begins with a simple meditation and develops into a joyful collective dance where each villager adds thoughts and ideas to the cauldron of rhythms. As his song titles suggest, McCoy's music is always powerfully metaphorical and easy to relate to a visual image. Listen to some more McCoy—"Blues on the Corner" from *The Real McCoy* (1967) or "Utopia" from *Tender Moments* (1968)—and you'll have the same sense of a powerfully communicative and articulate musical voice.

Lee Morgan, "Ca-Lee-So," from <u>Delightfulee</u> (1966)

Remember what we said about trumpet players? Cocky, brash, and born bandleaders? In an approachable, appealing kind of way, Lee Morgan epitomizes that stereotype. His music is far from egocentric or self-serving, and he was never the kind of musician to "beaugard" the gig away from the gifted musicians with whom he regularly performed. He was in fact highly in demand as a sideman. Still, Lee had that kind of take-charge sound that dominated the ensembles of which he was a part. If McCoy or Wayne played music that was introspective or spiritual, Lee was the classic extrovert who made jazz fans out of otherwise oblivious listeners.

The jazz community first noticed Morgan as the gifted teenage prodigy from Pittsburgh who shined in Dizzy Gillespie's big band. Subsequent stints with Art Blakey's Jazz Messengers in the late '50s and early to middle '60s established Morgan, along with a few others, as the inheritor of Clifford Brown's mantle as *the* postbop trumpet player. Typically bluesy and accessible, Morgan won considerable commercial success with a funky boogaloo entitled "The Sidewinder" that found its way onto a TV ad. As commercially visible as he became—and he is now often sadly neglected by listeners as a serious improviser—Morgan remained a consummate artist, and his tragic shooting in 1971 deprived jazz fans of one of the music's brightest stars.

"Ca-Lee-So," from Morgan's classic album *Delightfulee*, reflects

Lee's fascination with foreign rhythms. As a member of Blakey's band, he had experienced the African beats and grooves that the drummer was so fond of, and now he sought out the sounds of West Indian Calypso rhythms. Morgan was typically a forceful, aggressive player with an absolutely enormous tone and a swagger to his lines, but he reflects in the liner notes on how the different rhythms led him to adopt a more measured approach: "I'd been listening to the various Latin rhythms and noticing how popular bossa nova had become, so I thought I'd try something along these lines. It opens up a sort of new idiom for me; I find that the way this music flows, I tend to use space more, and use pretty lines instead of just running notes." Typically, jazz musicians consider different rhythmic influences, such as Brazilian bossa nova and Caribbean calypso, under the same "Latin" rubric.

"Ca-Lee-So," a not-so-subtle play on the trumpeter's first name on an album entitled *Delightfulee*, begins with the rhythm section grooving to a calypso rhythm. McCoy, now a sideman and in a much more light-hearted frame of mind, plays a singsong pattern to the accompaniment of Billy Higgins on drums and Bob Cranshaw on bass. One of the most ubiquitous drummers on the jazz scene since the '60s, "smiling Billy" wears a perpetual grin when he plays. His West Indian beat is actually a bastardized swing beat with Latin-tinged accents. If you listen closely to his trademark cymbal beat, you'll hear how he adapts a basic spang-a-lang into an infectious Caribbean groove.

After the sixteen-bar intro, Lee and tenor saxophonist Joe Henderson play Lee's melody. "Ca-Lee-So" is a simple thirty-two-bar, AABA form whose A sections are based on George Gershwin's "I Got Rhythm." As we discussed earlier, "rhythm changes," like the twelve-bar blues, are an adaptable and pervasive song form and the most standard of standards. Lee's "Ca-Lee-So" is but one of hundreds of jazz compositions that draw on Gershwin's simple harmonies, and even other calypso pieces, like trumpeter Blue Mitchell's "Fungi Mama," similarly use Gershwin's changes as base material. During the bridge, which departs from the standard rhythm-changes harmonies, note how Higgins shifts rhythms and cymbal beats to accommodate the syncopated melody. Harmonically simple, "Ca-Lee-So" derives its personality from its funky islands melody, which sounds like a line Lee might have improvised on the spot.

Lee's solo incorporates many of the elements that made him such a sought-after recording artist. Blessed with a huge, brassy sound, Morgan had the kind of virtuosic control over his instrument most people wish they had over their own voices. Indeed, Lee's sound is very vocal, infused with loud declarations and laughing smears. Check out the opening of his solo. His first eight bars are built around a simple two-note phrase, but at the end of that first A, he concludes with a sarcastic smear and crushed note. Never very far from the blues, he then shoots upward with a characteristically funky phrase. Throughout his solo, he almost sounds as if he's being deliberately and facetiously polite, holding his exuberance in check while he dances around the calypso rhythms. Morgan's music was often festive, but, as he suggested in the liner notes, whereas he might otherwise have more volubly "run lines" over the changes, on "Ca-Lee-So" he lays back, leaves a little space, and "plays pretty."

The restlessly creative Joe Henderson follows Morgan with two choruses that are spectacularly coherent. Joe was and is a powerful composer and bandleader in his own right. His Blue Note albums from the '60s—such as *Inner Urge* and *Mode for Joe*—are some of the masterpieces from the label's catalog, and he has continued to make superb albums for a number of other record companies. Joe falls somewhere on the spectrum between Wayne and Trane. He blends the latter's urgency with the former's intellect and shares a penchant for unpredictability, soft one moment, agitated the next.

Joe's "Ca-Lee-So" solo is a perfect example of musical architecture, thoughtfully organized but also passionate and swinging. The entire solo spins out of Joe's opening phrase, a descending three-note pattern that he toys with throughout most of his first chorus. During the mid-'60s, Joe added to his warm sound a slight edge and gruffness that contributed to the rhythmic impact of his lines. Along with his fervid vibrato, that slight growl enhances the party atmosphere of his "Ca-Lee-So" solo. After Joe twists his way through the rest of the next chorus, he concludes his statement with a return to the three-note phrase, coming full circle to complete his brief Caribbean essay.

The McCoy Tyner of "Ca-Lee-So" sounds far removed from the composer and improviser of "African Village." McCoy's solo here is less about density, power, and drama and more about settling into the comfortable groove established by Higgins and Cranshaw. McCoy's musical personality is still in evidence, nonetheless. His ringing attack remains, as does his focus on rhythm. Like most great sidemen, McCoy naturally adapts to the musical context without suppressing his basic musical voice. Here, he sustains the playful vibe established by Lee and Joe, and, by his second chorus, plays alongside Higgins as percussionist, accenting and punching his way through the calypso feel.

Indeed, the rhythmic feel of "Ca-Lee-So" is what makes the entire performance so memorable. Whatever the particular vocabulary of Morgan, Henderson, or Tyner, it is the essential groove of Higgins and Cranshaw that propels the whole piece. As I've stated time and again, rhythm, however conceived, helps define the jazz sound. "Ca-Lee-So" is a great example of how jazz musicians take an alternative rhythmic feel, here from the West Indies, and make it swing.

Herbie Hancock, "Maiden Voyage," from Maiden Voyage (1965)

Before reading any farther, cue up Herbie Hancock's "Maiden Voyage" on your CD player and listen; tune in without any prompting or explanation from this book or other critical voices. Just close your eyes and experience the sound and vibe of Herbie's music. "Maiden Voyage" sounds . . . relaxed . . . ethereal or maybe a little spacy . . . almost futuristic, awash in an unknown sea. A first voyage into uncharted but friendly territory. You are certainly in a far different zone from the traditional groove of Art Blakey's "Blues" or Sonny Clark's "Speak Low," and the intensity—quiet and inward—is nothing like McCoy's riotous "African Village." As tenor saxophonist George Coleman, trumpeter Freddie Hubbard, and Hancock proceed with three very different solos, that otherworldly vibe expands.

Now go back to the beginning of the track and play it again, thinking in more musical terms and listening for the devices jazz musicians use. Why does this piece sound so different from the others we've heard? Check out the eight-bar rhythm section intro and drummer Tony Williams's cymbal beat, played roughly in unison with piano and bassist Ron Carter. The groove is different—neither spang-a-lang, nor overtly African, nor Caribbean—and incredibly relaxed and loose. Moreover, there is a repeating rhythmic pattern or vamp here that the rhythm section plays throughout the head and during most of the solos. The long tones of the melody and the chord changes move up and down enigmatically, but the rhythmic vamp remains steady and grounded throughout.

The rhythmic feel of "Maiden Voyage" is an elusive one indeed, and it both springs and departs from many different traditions. In one oversimplified sense, "Maiden Voyage" has an implied "straight eighths" feel, meaning that the drummer plays straight and continuous eighth notes rather than the syncopated swing beat. In other words, instead of "spang, spang-a-lang, spang-a-lang," the cymbal spells out an insistent pulse of "da-da, da-da, da-da, da-da," with each "da-da" set representing one beat composed of two eighth notes. Straight eights are incorporated into Brazilian bossa-nova beats as well as basic rock rhythms.

Of course, in "Maiden Voyage" the straight eighths feel is at most implied, as the groove is broken down into syncopated parts by Herbie's rhythmic vamp. There is also a touch of funk in Herbie's vamp and bass line, but whereas funk or rock beats or even the typical straight eighths feels are indeed "straight" and locked in to a particular groove, the rhythm section here is supremely loose and unpredictable. Hancock, Williams, and Carter use the insistent pulse of the vamp as a flexible reference for rhythmic interplay and improvisation. The feel of "Maiden Voyage," reflecting jazz, Brazilian, and rock rhythms, is a classic example of the open-ended inclusiveness of the jazz musician's rhythmic repertoire.

Like sections of "African Village," "Maiden Voyage" is a modal piece built around the scales or modes suggested by its deceptively simple chord changes. Remember, a standard like "Speak Low" or rhythm changes or even a blues has a progression of chords with predictable relationships. Each chord naturally flows into the next by creating tensions that resolve inevitably into familiar harmonies. The ability to play certain standards translates often into the ability to play others, because so many standards have similar chord relationships.

Modal pieces like "Maiden Voyage" place different demands on the musician. Each mode or scale operates independently to suggest a certain sound, which may not resolve naturally into the next chord, if there even is one. Whereas standards require the discipline to navigate through numerous chord changes, modal pieces deprive you of the road map of those changes. You can't rely on your stock standards licks, but rather must create in the open field of a mode. You don't think this way when you play, of course—if you become too cognizant of what you are doing, the self-consciousness inhibits your performance—but the different material inevitably affects your expression. Without the signposts of predictable chord changes, the modal improviser is liberated to speak freely, but at the risk of losing focus.

Whereas the modal section in "African Village" is simply an open-ended E-minor vamp, the "modes" in "Maiden Voyage" are somewhat more structured by the traditional thirty-two-bar, AABA form of the tune. Yes, the unmistakably modern "Maiden Voyage" has the same overall form as Irving Berlin's ancient "Remember." The modes involved are based on four "suspended," or simply "sus," chords. Regardless of the technical meaning of a "suspended" chord, the designation is an apt one. Sus chords hover between minor and major sounds, between resolution and ambiguity, and their unresolved quality serves Herbie's future-oriented purpose well.

Harmonies aside, it is more than anything else the band's performance that ultimately gives "Maiden Voyage" its enduring vibe. Herbie's group on the album *Maiden Voyage* was actually identical to Miles Davis's quintet of the early '60s with trumpeter Freddie Hubbard substituted for Miles. No doubt Herbie chose the musicians he had performed with every night in clubs and concerts to ensure a loose familiarity in the studio. The greatness of Miles's band, many believe, began with the startling responsiveness and innovation of its rhythm section of Herbie, Ron, and Tony.

Along with Elvin Jones, Tony Williams was the most influential and radically inventive drummer of the postbop era, and his untimely death in early 1997 has left the jazz world bereft. Even as a teenager with Miles, Tony brought a new level of technical mastery and rhythmic command to the instrument. Check out his remarkable cymbal touch throughout "Maiden Voyage." Although he was one of the most explosively powerful percussionists in history—some say the loudest drummer ever—listen to how delicately Tony sketches rhythmic textures around the repeated vamp of the tune. Tony's trademark cymbals of that era, known by the brand name Zildjian Ks, are still a hallmark of the modern drum sound with their sense of being surrounded by so much "air." Key in on the dizzying variety of sounds and rhythmic ideas Tony conjures from his cymbals, hi-hat, toms, and snare. His accompaniment on an ostensibly nontonal instrument is as varied in color and texture as the most searching horn solo.

Williams's band mate with Miles, bassist Ron Carter, is the consummate modern bassist. As we heard on "Miyako," Carter is an unusually melodic and harmonically astute accompanist. What is so special about his performance on "Maiden Voyage" is how unobtrusively he locks in with and responds to the rest of the band. In one sense, he plays the traditional bass role of anchoring the ensemble by spelling out Herbie's rhythmic vamp and the basic chords of the piece. In another, his approach is radical as he departs from the primary chords and rhythms to respond to the soloist's needs. In and around the vamp he lays down, Ron double-stops, strums, and chases the soloists around. Somehow he manages to sustain the pulse and structure of the tune without freezing it up. Because he is so flexible and solid, the rest of the band can loosely explore the composition's possibilities.

Herbie rounds out the miracle rhythm section and is a strong presence well before he begins his solo. As we heard on "Miyako," Herbie is a melodic comper, with an endless supply of intriguing chord voicings to complement the soloist. And along with Tony and Ron, Herbie has the rare gift of being immediately responsive to where everyone else in the band is headed. Perhaps more than any piece we have listened to, "Maiden Voyage" captures the conversation among and around a brilliant rhythm section. One time through the cut, just focus on how the rhythm section supports and spurs the soloist, dynamically and telepathically shifting with every emphasis by the lead voice.

After the band states the melody of the tune, a simple two-phrase motif positioned and repositioned over the sus chords, George Coleman begins the soloing. Big George is a fixture on the current New York City jazz scene, and his quartet featuring piano virtuoso Harold Mabern serves almost as the city's house band. During so many of the nights I played and listened at Bradley's, George disappeared from the bar for a few moments, only to reappear with his tenor and humiliate other pretenders on the gig. Now an old pro, at the time of "Maiden Voyage" George was a young lion, serving time in Miles's band before Wayne took over.

George plays one eloquent chorus on Herbie's tune. Notice how wildly different his tenor sound is from that of Hank Mobley, Trane, Newk, or Wayne. Critics have described it as "keening" or "pinched." Whatever you hear in Big George's sound, his breathy fluidity fits the airy, dream-induced vibe of Herbie's tune perfectly. George is also a master technician—he often insists on playing a given tune through all twelve keys—and he breezes deftly through Herbie's changes. By the bridge, he is doubling up, just as we heard Trane and Mobley do earlier. George's confident mastery of the instrument is apparent in these thirty-two bars.

Freddie Hubbard ("Hub") follows on trumpet with a dynamically schizophrenic solo. Freddie, like Lee Morgan, has the swagger and confidence of most top trumpet players. His warm sound, the clarity of his lines, and his reputation as one of the most naturally swinging of modern improvisers have established Freddie as arguably the greatest trumpet player alive today. Less earthy and maybe slicker than Lee Morgan, Freddie nonetheless combines Morgan's brashness with Clifford Brown's relaxed swing.

Freddie's two-chorus "Maiden Voyage" solo is one of those rare mo-

ments of studio recording that rivals the spontaneity of live performance. His first eight bars are quiet and contemplative; he eases softly
into his solo as Herbie, Ron, and Tony overlay a new rhythmic pattern
on the basic vamp of the tune. Hub quickly opens up, however, and
begins his second A with a declaratory statement in the upper register.
Just as he gathers steam, he recedes into introspection again for the
bridge and the final A of his first chorus. He quiets the band down to a
near-total silence. Like Wayne Shorter, he is being quietly revealing and
holding his power and chops in reserve.

By the beginning of his next chorus, Freddie speaks out again, this
time doubling up and reveling in the precision and clarity of his phrasing. The reserve with which he began is now replaced by his irrepressible
spirit as an improviser. By the next bridge, Freddie is fluttering up and
down the range of the horn, and the rhythm section simply floats, lets
the rhythmic pulse of the tune deliberately fall apart. That bridge is a
fascinating moment of organized chaos, where everyone speaks at once
in a quiet melee. But in keeping with the spirit of the whole solo, the
band eases back into the tune's groove and pulse at the end of Hub's
solo. In two experimental choruses, Freddie ranges from pensive to righ-
teous to shy to brash to tremulous.

Herbie begins his solo in singsong fashion, exploring different ways
to voice and reharmonize the chords of "Maiden Voyage." Herbie, who
can conjure up the same kind of wild intensity McCoy does, was also a
great admirer of Bill Evans, one of his predecessors in Miles's band.
Evans was an unabashed romantic, who brought a classical sense of
harmonic freedom to standards. You can hear that influence in Herbie's
"Maiden Voyage" solo. Herbie is less concerned here with the single
note lines of bop masters like Wynton Kelly—another of Hancock's
chief influences and precursors in Miles's band—or the clusters and
clangs of Monk. His romanticism here evokes more of Ravel and Debussy and other European influences. Some "east of the border" harmonies combined with "south of the border" rhythms.

Herbie's solo just might be the best example of true group improvisation we have heard. He moves in and out of different moods as Freddie did, although not with the same schizophrenic blur, and Ron and

Tony follow suit. Herbie's solo is really more of a dialogue among the rhythm section. Indeed, in a fashion similar to Freddie's solo, Herbie, Ron, and Tony lapse into total rhythmic freedom during Herbie's second bridge. Herbie runs "arpeggios," the splintered notes of a chord, up and down the keyboard like a classical pianist as Tony and Ron brood out of time. The metaphor we used earlier of the current of a river was never more appropriate; the underlying flow and pulse of the tune move inexorably forward even as countercurrents, eddies, and waves wash over the surface. Then, gently, Herbie glides back into the tune's basic vamp and the horns state the melody one final time.

Jazz embraces outside influences but then crafts them to serve its own needs. Lee Morgan and Billy Higgins take a calypso rhythm and make it swing in the best jazz tradition. McCoy takes the sounds and images of Africa and co-opts them into his utopian vision of how a jazz waltz might sound. In "Maiden Voyage," Herbie combines Brazilian rhythms and European harmonies into a forward-looking vehicle for open improvisation. The groove and swing are always there—that's why it's jazz—but they enter from different ports into this American art form.

Francis Wolff/Mosaic Images

Ornette Coleman

Rehearsal for Empty Fox Hole *session*
1966

Out

11

IT'S TIME TO take things "out." Playing "out"—or being "out," for that matter—means departing from convention, operating outside the usual and expected parameters. If a bass player is personally "out," he's a little weird or offbeat, maybe spaced-out or just plain crazy. The description can be affectionate or pejorative, depending upon the open-mindedness of the speaker and the degree of craziness involved. An "out" gig in the negative sense is usually a mess of some sort; either the band just couldn't get it together musically, or the sound man botched the mikes, or the club owner hassled you about the money.

Playing "out" or "outside" can mean that you are playing a standard, such as "Green Dolphin Street," and you choose lines that conflict conspicuously with the chord changes of the tune. You have reached outside its expected confines. We've heard some outness already. Chick's "Matrix" certainly took an outside approach to something as rudimentary as the blues, and McCoy and Bobby strayed far and wide from the E-minor chord in "African Village" 's vamp sections. You might not think of "Maiden Voyage" as out at first blush, but Herbie's solo certainly overstepped the boundaries of the composition's harmonies and rhythms.

But what happens if you take things really out? Suppose you dispense with chord changes or modes altogether? Imagine no song form, chord structure, choruses, or set number of bars. What if you don't even maintain a steady beat but let rhythms sway back and forth with no anchoring pulse? You get "free jazz," where everything is "out," where improvisers are liberated from the dictates of harmony and rhythm. Most of the great modern players have experimented with such freedom in one way or another. On various Blue Note records by Freddie Hubbard, Bobby Hutcherson, Chick Corea, Wayne Shorter, Herbie Hancock, and a host of others, one or two tunes exploit that total freedom.

Free jazz, the essence of playing out, is associated with the avant-garde. If improvised music in general has a hard time attracting new listeners, free jazz can occasionally be painfully inaccessible. Pianist Cecil Taylor, who treats the piano like a large percussion box, is several steps beyond the "where's the melody?" crowd. Some of Trane's later explorations, where he adds drummer Rashied Ali and saxophonist Pharaoh Sanders to his already incendiary quartet, are almost unlistenable in their intensity. I love that music. You may discover that you do too, but you certainly have to be in a different frame of mind to enjoy it.

Free jazz, however, is not necessarily more remote. Many of Miles's classic mid-'60s Columbia albums—*The Sorcerer* and *Nefertiti*, for instance—feature free music. The band would play one of Wayne's elliptical melodies and then solo freely, with only a suggestion of that melody as a foundation. Out indeed, but those recordings are some of the most swinging in modern jazz history. Trane's open-ended ballads are equally free, but they have an emotional immediacy that most singers of conventional ballads should strive for. The challenge is to tame the freedom and make it musical. Let's check in with the master, Ornette Coleman, and hear a sample of how he did it.

Ornette Coleman, "Round Trip," from New York Is Now! (1969)

Alto saxophonist Ornette Coleman is the father of free jazz. By the end of the '50s, Ornette had already comfortably dispensed with chord structures and time signatures. His famous dirge, "Lonely Woman," released in 1959, was a somber, impassioned drone without a clear pulse. His alarming "Free Jazz," recorded in 1960, liberated two quartets to improvise collectively and wildly. When I first heard "Free Jazz," I thought maybe the band was just tuning up, like an orchestra in a Broadway pit before the audience trails in. The group, which included pioneers like Freddie Hubbard and Eric Dolphy, in fact never plays deliberately in tune at all!

But while Ornette is a forward-looking revolutionary, his music is also some of the most earthy and elemental we'll hear. As radical as it may have seemed to leave structure and conventional harmony aside, Ornette was just trying to break down emotional barriers to his expressiveness. If you are truly going to speak your mind through your instrument, why limit your vocabulary by adhering to predetermined structures? Why not simply play, express joy or sadness or furor or peace unfettered by musical convention? Ornette did not even play consistently in tune, but rather bent notes up and down into "microtones"—pitches that fall between the notes of a conventional scale. Why restrict yourself to the ordinary scales of the piano keyboard?

The irony is that this avant-garde approach is in many senses a simplification and a harking back. Pieces like Wayne Shorter's "Miyako" and Herbie's "Maiden Voyage" are dense, replete with sophisticated harmonies and rhythmic variations. Similarly, Hank Mobley's and Sonny Clark's bop lines are intricate in the way they closely track and alter standard harmonies. Ornette's approach may be avant-garde, but it's decidedly less cerebral. He's not interested in intricacy or harmonic complexity. His music shies away from formal theory and embraces an earlier tradition of blues and, as one critic noted, "field hollers."

New York Is Now! captures Ornette after he was a longtime fixture on the jazz scene. His band for the date, different from his working ensemble of the time, included two-thirds of Trane's famous rhythm section, bassist Jimmy Garrison and drummer Elvin Jones, as well as tenor saxophonist Dewey Redman on the front line. By 1969, free jazz was no longer a shocking concept, but Ornette had burnished and perfected it as an approach to modern improvisation and had found a soul mate in Redman, as he had earlier in trumpeter Don Cherry.

"Round Trip" is vintage Ornette. The head has some simple suggested harmonies that Jimmy Garrison more or less implies on the bass, but it is mostly just a simple, folksy melody. The ensemble sound here is far different from anything else we've heard. First, there's no piano, much less a guitar or other chordal instrument. If you're not going to play chord changes, why have a pianist's chord voicings intrude? The pianoless group was not an unheard-of instrumentation; Gerry Mulligan on the West Coast and Newk in the East often led bands without that third of the rhythm section. But for Ornette, the absence of the piano was fundamental. It freed him up to go anywhere he, bass, and drums might choose.

Listen also to how Dewey and Ornette state the melody of "Round Trip" lazily, almost sloppily. In Sonny's Clark's "Speak Low," Wayne's "Miyako, and Lee's "Ca-Lee-So," the horns play tightly together like one unit; any intonation problems would have stood out awkwardly. Ornette and Dewey, in contrast, don't strive to play exactly together rhythmically or to control their intonation in equivalent ways. The goal is not to sound tightly knit and "conducted," but rather loosely expressive.

After the brief head, Ornette is off and running. Unlike some of his freer pieces, "Round Trip" does have a pulse and a time signature, and Elvin and Jimmy start walking and swinging in a traditional spang-a-lang immediately after the melody. Beyond the four/four swing groove, however, the performance is totally free, with no chord changes, sections, or form. Even more than modal pieces, free tunes like "Round Trip" pose a unique challenge to the improviser, for there is no obvious frame of reference on which to base the solo. Standards have familiar chord relationships, and even harmonically daring pieces like "Miyako" suggest certain melodies to the soloist. Modal compositions are more open-ended but still provide modes or scales as a foundation. Remember earlier we talked about chord progressions and song forms as the "organizing principle"? The free improviser does not have that cushion.

Ornette's solo on "Round Trip" is nonetheless as orderly as anything we've heard. For him, melody is central. Even if there are no predictable chords or eight-bar sections, he crafts his solo around melodic fragments. In fact, from the opening moments of his solo, he plays a simple motif and then explores its possibilities all over the horn. So many of the horn players we have heard similarly toyed with musical phrases, but for Ornette, motific development is a science that lends order to an otherwise amorphous form.

Note also that Ornette's solo, free as it is, doesn't sound particularly atonal or aggressively "out." Without actually spelling out chord changes, Ornette keeps roughly to a major scale in the sort-of key signature of the song. He plays in and out of time, sometimes rushing ahead of the beat and other times relaxing into the swing feel, but always referring back to the melodic phrase with which he began his solo. Again, there is something very elemental about his approach, something far more rudimentary and gritty than other solo styles we have heard. "Round Trip" is a bright, happy-sounding tune, and the organizing principle of Ornette's solo is simply that mood itself.

After Ornette completes his initial statement, Dewey Redman takes over with a breathy urgency in his tenor sound. Father to young star Joshua Redman, Dewey is a sorcerer of free music. Like Ornette, he begins his solo by dissecting a melodic fragment. Check out how Jimmy and Elvin follow Dewey as he descends into what musicians like to call some "nebulae"—space time. Jimmy begins strumming a repeated drone on the bass, and Elvin, who remained pretty laid back during Ornette's solo, begins to loosen and break down the swing feel as Dewey rolls around the bottom register and then squawks up high. The band returns briefly to a walking feel, but that, too, quickly rends apart at the seams when bass and drums begin a stop-start accompaniment.

Dewey and Ornette have very different approaches to playing free, at least during this particular performance. Ornette is congenial, happy to cavort in the major sounds of the head in keeping with the upbeat tone of the piece. Dewey's solo is much less "in." He draws on every note in the Western scale and even some notes in between, and explores every nuance of rhythm and sound. He slides up and down the horn in a kind of improvised stream of consciousness, and midway through his solo, he starts growling, crying, and squeaking. His solo is no longer simply about the notes he chooses or the tone of his tenor, but about the panoply of sounds and even noises he can get through the horn.

To complete the soloing, Ornette joins Dewey for a final, collective romp. Soloing together was very much part of Ornette's concept. It was the final abandonment of musical formality, for in addition to dispensing with chords and forms, he balked at the tradition of soloing in turns. Listen to the dialogue between Dewey and Ornette during the last third of "Round Trip": call and response, question and answer, squeak up high and rasp down low. Rather than getting in each other's way, Dewey and Ornette inspire and egg each other on to new ideas.

Finally, listen closely to Elvin and Jimmy throughout the track. Like the best accompanists, they both respond and prod, follow the horns and lead them upward. On records with Trane, Elvin and Jimmy are necessarily thunderous, if only to meet the intensity of the saxophonist's musical vision. With Ornette and Dewey, Elvin and Jimmy are a little lighter and looser. Ornette's earthiness, Dewey's watery miasma of notes, and the tidy chaos of the collective soloing all elicit a sympathetic response from bass and drums. What they do so well is to capture the unconfined swell of the piece without ever losing sight of the beat that makes even this freedom swing hard.

"Round Trip" and the music it typifies were a necessary next step for the improvisers we have been hearing. It's not surprising that after solving the puzzles of bop and perfecting the dense harmonies of Herbie, Wayne, and Miles, some artists would seek to shake the confines of musical structure. That evolution parallels developments in other art forms. Nineteenth- and twentieth-century painting moved from exact replication to suggestion to total abstraction. Twentieth-century literature evolved into the likes of James Joyce, whose *Ulysses* eschewed the rules of grammar. Ornette did much the same. Forget the chord changes and AABA and playing in tune. Later for musical grammar. If I am to be freely articulate and directly expressive, let me just speak my language.

Ten tunes wouldn't do justice to even one of the artists we've heard, and we've heard only a fraction of the best of one very limited era. Even from the '50s and '60s, we haven't heard Bird or Miles or Trane with his quartet. What's more, except for the live Blakey tune, we've listened only to studio recordings, which are just one snapshot of an improviser's imagination in a necessarily artificial environment. What must it have been like to see Trane or Monk live, to see the first edition of Blakey's Jazz Messengers or Ornette or Miles as they broke new ground? Outside the confines or a recording studio and with the inspiration of a living and engaged audience, it must have been outrageous.

The outrageous stuff is still happening every day. Jazz is alive and kicking in clubs, lofts, and concert halls throughout the world. There are young phenoms and revered elder statesmen. There are debates over who's too conservative, who doesn't know the tradition, what's creative, and what's hype. At the Vanguard, it might be an eighty-year-old tenor player leading a roaring big band, while down the street at Sweet Basil or at Blues Alley in D.C., an alto player squawks his way through a modern abstraction. Ornette's got a new record, you just heard an astounding eighteen-year-old pianist, and there's a stream of reissues of classic '30s and '40s recordings. Go to the record stores and the clubs, check out the music, and see where your preferences lie.

With ten tunes under your belt, you now have a little more familiarity with the way jazz works. You know what a rhythm section is and what a swing beat sounds like. You've heard the wildly different sounds two players can extract from the same tenor saxophone or drums. You've got some sense of the repertoire, of standards and blues and free music. You've started to learn the language of jazz. Now it's time to go out and join the conversation.

INDEX

Rodney, Red, 65
Rodgers, Richard, 80
Roker, Mickey, 72
Rolling Stones, 82
Rollins, Sonny ("Newk"), xiv, 23, 57–58, 59, 60, 67, 84, 93, 118, 132, 136, 145, 152
  ballads, 125–29
Roney, Wallace, 93
Rosnes, Renee, 93
Rosolino, Frank, 70
"Round Midnight," 78, 86, 125
"Round Trip," 150–54
Rouse, Charlie, 87
"Ruby, My Dear," 86, 125
Russell, Curly, 106, 110, 116

Sahara, 134
"St. Thomas," 132
Sanders, Pharaoh, 150
"Satin Doll," 85
Saxophone, 4, 52–61, 69, 102, 103
Scatting, 75
Schizophrenia, 121–24
Scofield, John, 71
Scott, Shirley, 74
"Search for Peace," 134
"Senor Blues," 87
Set list, xiii, 77–88
Shaw, Artie, 69
Shaw, Woody, 67–68, 70, 74, 88, 112, 113, 132, 145, 146, 150, 154
Shearing, George, 47
Shorter, Wayne, 16, 45, 51–52, 53, 60, 66, 69, 70, 73, 78, 79, 83, 92, 136, 138, 140, 145, 146, 150, 154
  ballads, 120, 121–24, 127, 128, 134, 151, 152
  radicalism, 87–88
Shuffles, 23, 25
"Sidewinder, The," 138
Silver, Horace, 87, 95, 110, 112–13, 116, 137
Sinatra, Frank, 81
Singers, 74–75
"Single Petal of a Rose," 85
"Skippy," 87, 126
Smalls (club), 99
Smith, Jimmy, 71, 74, 109
Smith, Lonnie, 74
Smithsonian Collection of Classic Jazz, The, 92
Snare drum, 39–40, 41, 42
"So What," 65
Solos/soloists, xiv, 7, 9, 12
  bassist and/as, 36, 37
  collective, 154
  drums, 42
  free jazz, 150
  piano, 46, 47, 48

"Some Other Stuff," 70
Something Else, 83
Song, underlying, 7, 9
"Song for My Father," 87, 113
Song form/structure, 18, 22, 30
  blues, 108
  improvising on, 78–79
  as organizing principle, 152
Song of the New World, 134
Sonny's Crib, 99–105
"Sophisticated Lady," 85
Soprano sax, 53
Sorcerer, The, 150
Soul Station, 94–99, 100
Sound
  bassist, 34–35
  Coltrane, 58–59
  rhythm and, 141
  trumpet, 62–63
Spang-a-lang, 14, 21–26, 40
Spaulding, James, 69, 122
"Speak Low," 99–105, 122, 132, 141, 142, 152
Sphere, 87
Standards, 16, 65, 68, 78, 80–84, 143, 152
  ballads, 120
  jazz, 85, 88
  reharmonizing, 48
Standards album, 83–84
"Stella by Starlight," 99
Stewart, Slam, 32
Stop time, 112, 113
"Straight No Chaser," 108
Strayhorn, Billy, 16, 85, 120
Stride piano tradition, 47–48, 125–26
Sun Ship, 103, 119
"Survival Blues," 134
"Sweet Papa Lou," 111
Swing, 14, 21–24, 64, 66, 71, 92, 94, 147
  as relaxed intensity, 24–26
  among vocalists, 75
Swing beat, 22, 23, 26, 39, 41, 155

"Take the A Train," 85
Tatum, Art, 13, 48
Taylor, Art ("A.T."), 40, 100, 101, 104–5, 116, 132
Taylor, Cecil, 150
Tempo, 13, 42
Tenor saxophone, xiii, 44, 54, 56–58, 60–61
Terry, Clark, 67, 75
Think of One, 68
Thirty-two-bar form, 18
Thompson, Lucky, 57
Time for Tyner, 133–38
Time signature, 14
Timmons, Bobby, 109
"Tom Thumb," 121